DANCING
WITH WORDS

DANCING WITH WORDS

Signing for Hearing Children's Literacy

Marilyn Daniels

BERGIN & GARVEY
Westport, Connecticut • London

Library of Congress Cataloging-in-Publication Data

Daniels, Marilyn.
  Dancing with words : signing for hearing children's literacy / by Marilyn Daniels.
    p. cm.
  Includes bibliographical references and index.
  ISBN 0–89789–723–4 (alk. paper)—ISBN 0–89789–792–7 (pbk. : alk. paper)
    1. Sign language.   2. American Sign Language.   3. Literacy.   4. Language acquisition.
  5. Language arts (Elementary)   I. Title.
  HV2474.D25   2001
  419'.0973—dc21   00–027239

British Library Cataloguing in Publication Data is available.

Library of Congress Catalog Card Number: 00–027239
ISBN: 0–89789–723–4
       0–89789–792–7 (pbk.)

First published in 2001

Bergin & Garvey, 88 Post Road West, Westport, CT 06881
An imprint of Greenwood Publishing Group, Inc.
www.greenwood.com

Printed in the United States of America

∞

The paper used in this book complies with the
Permanent Paper Standard issued by the National
Information Standards Organization (Z39.48–1984).

10 9 8 7 6 5 4 3 2

Copyright Acknowledgments

The author and the publisher gratefully acknowledge permission for use of the following
material:

The poem "A Visit with a Whale," by Ginny Buckingham. Used with permission of Ginny
Buckingham.

Student reactions to using sign language in their sixth grade class. Reactions recorded by their
teacher Marie Carmichael for the purpose of being included in this volume. Used with permission of Marie Carmichael.

for Tony

Contents

Part IV   Doing It

Acknowledgments

There are many people to thank who have contributed to this work and the research on which it is based. It seems to me that it all started when inquisitive students, in a communication theory class I was teaching at Central Connecticut State University, in New Britain, Connecticut, asked me, "Why should hearing children of deaf parents, coming out of home environments where they are encountering very little English, be demonstrating above-average ability in their English language arts?" I answered that I did not know why, and that they were correct in thinking that it did not make logical sense. So I begin with an acknowledgment of these curious students, who sent me on my initial quest to discover the answer to their question.

The first research study I directed on this topic was conducted in Pennsylvania at the Scranton State School for the Deaf (SSSD). The Deaf community and the school staff were supportive of an endeavor they didn't quite understand, and they helped me locate hearing children whose Deaf parents used American Sign Language as the native language in the home. Arnine Weiss and Marge Marino facilitated my communication with the parents of the studies' participants, for at that time, I knew very little sign language. Particular thanks must go to the SSSD Director, Dorothy Baumbach, and Debra Maltese, North East Regional Director for the Pennsylvania State Office for Deaf and Hearing Impaired. To Vicki Ferrance, Laura Ann Dumback,

Annette Chapman, Sandra Pastore, Nancy Jo Gilboy, Ellen Exner, Debbie Fitewater, Nancy Powell, Chris Dumback, Robert Redno, and Pam Diamond, the parents of the initial signing cohort, my appreciation for their effort and cooperation. And thanks also to Winfield McChord, Jr., Executive Director, American School for the Deaf, in West Hartford, Connecticut, who kindly opened his records to me during the early stages of the research.

It may seem curious to thank Oliver Sacks at this point, but I do, for it is through his book *Seeing Voices* that I came to a deeper understanding of sign language and became aware of some research initiatives that were taking place in Prince George's County, Maryland. Through the auspices of the late Judy Hoyer, who was the Director of Early Childhood Education in the county, I made contact with several teachers who were using sign language as part of their instructional practices. These teachers and their students acted as treatment classes, and other teachers and their students served as control classes for a number of my initial research studies with typical hearing students. I thank Patty Lambrecht, Mary Pullen, Pat Wilson, Diane Citron, and Inez Saddler for their contributions.

Special recognition is due Bob Wilson, Jan Hafer and Cindy Bowen. They came to know about my research through Judy Hoyer, who suggested me as a keynote speaker for an International Reading Association Conference held in Baltimore County, Maryland, in 1993. I am indebted to all of the Baltimore County teachers who have worked with me on research since that time. They are Ginny Buckingham, Virginia Whalen, Patty Nestor, Jeanne Blades, Lynn Float, Cathy Cunningham, Kathy Powell, Joyce Apgar, Maggie Syndor, Anita Benjamin, Jean Mattheiss, and Shirley Makin.

I acknowledge the financial support I have received from a series of Research Development Grants funded by the Pennsylvania State University. These grants made it possible for me to conduct the research over a large geographic region during an extended time frame. Ultimately both factors engendered finer research because they enabled me to broaden the socioeconomic base and discover whether the educational gains were maintained over time.

Next, my thanks goes to the United Kingdom Sign in Education project team and its developer, Kathy Robinson; to Laura Feltzer and Ruth Nishida in California; Diane Dennis, Paul Kazmierowicz, and his children, Alexandra and Jessica, in Oregon; Carol Analco in Michigan; Geri Litzen in Alaska; Sue E. Maribito and Bonnie Jean Polley in New Hampshire; Maywood Giordano, Joan Lundeen, Jayme Maloney, Anne Potter, and Marie Carmichael in Vermont; and Donovan Buterakos and his mother, Kathleen Buterakos, in Virginia.

The unnamed parents, principals, school secretaries, and other administrators who facilitated the adoption and acceptance of the research projects and made the day-to-day operation of the studies and the related evaluation processes advance so smoothly have earned my gratitude through their tireless efforts.

Finally, my gratitude to all the children who have participated in these research endeavors since 1991. They have numbered nearly five hundred. They have been cooperative, patient, and dear, and I thank them. The research is ultimately for them. Helping children achieve knowledge, comfort, and pleasure while dancing with words has always been the goal.

PART I

Getting Started

_____ Chapter I _____

Introduction

This book is about sign language and how sign language can be used to improve hearing children's English vocabulary, reading ability, spelling proficiency, self-esteem, and comfort with expressing emotions. Sign also facilitates communication, is an effective tool for establishing interaction between home and school, aids teachers with classroom management, has been shown to promote a more comfortable learning environment and initiates an interest in and enthusiasm for learning on the part of students. I know, it sounds like magic.

Within the pages of this book you will encounter hard facts, research reports, and historical evidence that demonstrate that the claims delineated in the preceding paragraph are true. You will be able to read the reactions of children, parents, and teachers who have used sign language for educational purposes. You will be shown how to begin to use sign language at home with your own children or how to incorporate it in curriculum in a classroom setting. The book is written for both parents and teachers who would like to enhance children's education with sign language.

The book is organized in four parts: Getting Started, Research, Theory, and Doing It. In this first introductory chapter, of Part I, Getting Started, you will find a fairly complete explanation of the material covered in each of the various parts. Depending on your background and personal perspective you may choose to read the chapters in your own order, and there may be some chapters that hold no particular interest for you. Skip these and feel free to approach the text as it appears to make the most sense for you, on the basis of your own knowledge and needs.

Part I, Getting Started, continues with the chapter on sign language, Chapter 2, which provides a short history of sign language and its primary use within the Deaf community. A number of variants of sign language are identified, and the difference between American Sign Language (ASL) and signing exact English (SEE) or pidgin signed English (PSE) is explained. The structure of ASL is defined and its four phonological features, location, handshape, movement, and orientation, are described. Sign language's use of space as well as its nonmanual features are explored. The discussion explains that individual ASL words do not always have exact English counterparts. Fingerspelling and the manual alphabet are covered. Chapter 3 concludes with linguists' recognition of ASL as an authentic language and its ever-growing acceptance as a foreign language in high schools and colleges, which has recently made it the third most common language in the United States.

Part I ends with Chapter 3. This is a chapter on reading, which explains exactly what reading is and how it differs from speech. The components of reading are identified and the steps to reading success are delineated with suggestions for incorporating sign language in the process in a timely learning fashion. The text is comprehensive, although I endeavor to remove as much jargon as possible in an effort to make the material easily accessible to more readers.

Part II, Research, begins with Chapter 4, the longest chapter in the book, which covers all of the research projects I have directed since 1991 concerning the use of sign language in typical hearing children's education. The positive results reported in these studies are the primary reason this book is written. After examining the entire body of my research you have some idea of the magnitude of statistical support for signs' benefit for hearing children's language development. Pulling it all together in one place is important for understanding the depth and breadth of the studies that have been conducted to date.

Part II continues with Chapter 5, which details the reactions of the student participants, the teachers, and the parents to the use of sign language in education. You can read what students wrote about their sign language experience. These firsthand accounts are charming and revealing as they point to a number of ancillary benefits the young learners describe that fall outside the purview of the specific educational aims of the particular sign project but apparently occurred and were worthwhile additions to their lives.

A portion of this chapter reveals the teachers' enthusiasm for and appreciation of the value of the addition of sign language instruction to the typical elementary school curriculum. In their quoted statements you can read about their personal experiences. They explain the preparation and effort expended in incorporating sign in their teaching, describing its attributes and advantages. The teachers are like a chorus all singing the same song of praise with no discordant notes. The chapter concludes as the parents chime in, with their comments supporting the observations of the teachers and the students. The beauty of all of these comments is that they represent the reactions of children, parents, and teachers from a variety of sign language programs involving different grade levels, in different geographic locations, with different racial and socioeconomic aspects. Yet their comments mirror each other and give the reader a solid comprehensive picture of signs' benefits.

Although I am probably the most prolific researcher in this field, I am not the only person conducting research in this area. Chapter 6 contains reports of the research of others concerning the use of sign for educational advantage with typical hearing students. These studies are described in some detail and are fully documented. For readers who are interested in consulting these articles directly a complete bibliography is included at the close of the chapter.

The group of hearing children who have benefited from sign for the longest amount of time are hearing children with special needs. Sign has long been used with hearing children with Down syndrome, with autism, and with other communicative impairments. Chapter 7 reviews these published studies and concludes with an account of a current endeavor involving Hmong students taking place in Pontiac, Michigan.

Chapter 8, the final chapter in Part II, examines three different inclusive programs: an elementary school in Alaska, a preschool in Louisiana, and a primary school in the United Kingdom. It features the story of a unique sign language project, Sign in Education, taking place in the United Kingdom. This educational initiative attempts to teach hearing children and Deaf children the national curriculum in an inclusive classroom. The interesting twist with Sign in Education is that a good deal of the teaching is done by a Deaf teacher using

British Sign Language. This teacher cannot speak English and communicates with the students, both Deaf and hearing, in sign language only. Amazingly, the hearing children are not only learning their ordinary studies properly but are also acquiring British Sign Language (BSL). This chapter recounts the components of an interesting program and opens a wider range of possibilities for the use of sign language in education in the United States.

Chapter 9, Why It Works, constitutes Part III, Theory. Here you will become familiar with the theoretical rationale for the advantage of sign language to hearing students. What happens in a physiological sense when students use sign language? Are both hemispheres of the brain involved? What about memory? Where is the sign language stored? When students produce sign language, is a different kind of memory created? Is the multisensory aspect very significant to learning? What about play, feelings, self-esteem: are they all involved? Does sign actually lessen conflict in the classroom and aid classroom management? This chapter provides extensive answers to all of these questions.

Part IV, Doing It, contains two chapters that explain how to use sign language in a specific setting for a particular purpose. Chapter 10 covers use of sign language to help children achieve literacy in school. It begins with some general suggestions for teacher preparation. The process of enhancing prekindergarten and kindergarten education with sign language is described and examples are provided. Classroom management is addressed next, and the chapter concludes with specific directions for teaching reading, spelling, and social studies with sign language.

Chapter 11 is designed for parents; it teaches them to use sign language with their children in the home. This instruction can begin at an early age, when the child is just a baby, and can continue into the school-age years. Using sign facilitates communication and enhances understanding within the family. The chapter closes with thoughts about the acquisition of language in general and points out the systemic connection of sign language with all other natural languages.

Now that the structure of the book has been explained in some detail, you have a clearer picture of its contents and design. As you can readily see, some topics will be of greater interest than others to different readers. Each chapter is written in a fairly free-standing fashion, so that readers can focus on the chapters that seem most relevant to their pursuits.

_____ **Chapter 2** _____

Sign Language

What is sign language? Where did it come from? Is it really a language? Is it the same all over the world? What is American Sign Language? How does fingerspelling fit in? What does the manual alphabet look like? Is a sign always made in the same way? What is manual English or signed English? Is sign language considered a foreign language? This chapter will strive to answer these questions.

HISTORY

Sign language is a term that refers to many languages that have evolved throughout the world in situations in which spoken language was not possible. In some instances, notably in monastic communities, periods of silence were observed. This precipitated a need for a silent form of communication among the monks, and there is a documented history of daily use of sign language and a manual alphabet in Benedictine communities since before the Renaissance.

Spoken language was often difficult for people who were deaf, particularly those who were prelingually deaf (deaf before they have acquired the ability to speak). Such individuals had a compelling need to use sign language for discourse to express ideas and desires and learn the thoughts and wishes of others. Within families and communities consisting of people who were deaf, sign language filled language needs in a normal and natural manner. In the midst of these neighborhoods, sign language developed and was not artificially taught.

Recorded events of the past show that whenever teachers have been utilized to teach the language of the majority culture to people who were deaf, for example, Pedro Ponce de León (1510?–1584) in Spain or Abbé Charles Michael de l'Epée (1712–1789) in France, the teachers first learned the natural sign language of the country from the pupils. After they acquired sign language, the teachers proceeded to teach their students the Spanish or French language and reading. These early teachers make it quite clear in their reports of their work that they did not invent or create sign language, but rather learned it from their students and used it to teach the language of the country, be it Spanish or French.

So, sign language is a natural language, which is strongly rooted in Deaf communities throughout the world. A *natural language* is a language with native users, who absorb it from birth and for whom it fulfills the diverse communicative needs of daily life. Actually, there are many sign languages in the world. In the same way that different countries have different spoken and written languages, they have different signed languages. Examples are American Sign Language, British Sign Language, and French Sign Language, to name but a few.

AMERICAN SIGN LANGUAGE

How different are these sign languages? They are quite different. American Sign Language is more like French Sign Language and less like British Sign Language. This statement undoubtedly reads like a misprint, but it is true, and the reason for the similarity is that Laurent Clerc, a Deaf Frenchman, was the primary teacher at the first permanent school for the deaf in the United States. The school, where sign language was formally established, now known as the American School for the Deaf, opened its doors in Hartford, Connecticut, in the spring of 1817.

Clerc had arrived in this country a scant eight months earlier in the company of Thomas Hopkins Gallaudet, who had recruited him from his teaching job at the National Institute for the Deaf in Paris. Gallaudet had been in Europe investigating the best methods for educating Deaf students prior to founding a school in America. He was impressed with the French school and the procedures he encountered and made a decision to emulate their system in a residential school for children who were deaf in New England. Gallaudet was initiated into the use of the manual alphabet and the French Sign Language by Clerc, who simultaneously learned English from Gallaudet.

This early French influence accounts for the considerable component of French Sign Language embedded in the fledgling American Sign Language and the fact that today American Sign Language has more in common with French Sign Language than it has with British Sign Language. The American School and its teaching practices had a strong impact on the Deaf community and the evolution of its language because the school became the mother school for sixty-four similar residential institutions in the United States, where its alumnae served as teachers and administrators.

Linguists have recognized since 1960 that American Sign Language is a bona fide language. It is a complete language with all the properties of other languages of the world, existing entirely in a visual-gestural modality. The structure of American Sign Language is different from the structure of English, and it has evolved independently of, and separately from, English. Like other languages, it is composed of symbols that can be combined in a specific rule-based manner to express meaning. An infant exposed to the language acquires it in the same sequential learning pattern displayed by any child learning their native language. It is a living language that continues to grow and develop with regional variations typical of natural languages everywhere.

STRUCTURE OF ASL

Phonology

In spoken language the basic units of sound that constitute a word are formed in the oral cavity by the vocal organs, the lips, tongue, and teeth. In speech the sounds are classified according to the place of articulation, the manner of articulation, and the attribute of being voiced or unvoiced. The phonological properties of American Sign Language (ASL) involve manual articulation and movement that are salient to the visual system. These gestural components are classified in four specific parts: the *location* in which a sign is produced, or the placement in relationship to the articulator's body (about twenty distinct locations); the *handshape*(s) used to form the sign (about forty distinct handshapes); the *movement* or motion of the hands from one point to another in the signing space; and the *orientation* of the hands or palms (about ten distinct orientations). These are the four phonological features linguists have traditionally used to describe ASL phonology.

Morphology

In English, word formation occurs by affixation, adding prefixes and suffixes to a word stem. This transpires in a sequential or linear manner. Examples of such English construction would be the addition of the morpheme-*s* to the end of a noun to make it plural and the placement of the bound morpheme-*ment* at the end of a verb such as *improve,* converting it into the noun *improvement.* ASL morphology occurs in a simultaneous rather than a sequential way. The sign stem is nested within active movement contours. For instance, when signing the verb *improve* there is a single slow movement; when it becomes the noun *improvement* a faster, more dynamic movement occurs. The simultaneous morphology of ASL distinguishes it from the affixation morphology commonly used in English.

Syntax

In English, the word order is customarily subject-verb-object. With few inflections to show grammatical relationships, word order becomes important in English. On the other hand, although ASL often uses a subject-verb-object sequence, because it also uses grammatical facial expressions, spatial syntax, and other nonmanual features, the subject-verb-object pattern does not dominate the language.

Often the most important information is placed at the beginning of the ASL sentence, regardless of its grammatical function within the sentence. This practice, called *topicalization,* permits the signer to focus initial attention on the sentence's central idea. Facial expressions may also be used at the beginning of a sentence to show negation or to indicate yes and no questions.

Space

A significant aspect of ASL is its use of space. There is no analogous space aspect present in English. In ASL, space is used for indicating various verb tenses and for indexing. The concept of tense is represented by an imaginary time line from behind the signer's body to the front of the signer's body. The past is represented by the space in back of the signer, the future is represented by the space in front of the signer, and the present by the space nearest to the signer's torso. A signer usually establishes a time frame, and the entire discourse from that point forward remains in that time frame until the signer changes the time frame.

Space is also used for indexing: A referent, a person or object, is placed in space and then referred to by the conversational partners by *indexing*, pointing or even glancing at the space where the referent has been placed.

Nonmanual Characteristics

In ASL, nonmanual cues function as intonation acts in a spoken language or as punctuation acts in a written language. Movements of the eyes, mouth, face, hand, and body posture are all nonmanual characteristics, which can be used for this purpose. For instance, the sentence "She is old" can be signed as a simple declarative sentence; by furrowing the brow and exaggerating the hand movement when *old* is signed, the signer can indicate "She is very, very old!; or by shaking the head in a negative manner while signing the affirmative "She is old" the signer alters the sentence and conveys a sarcastic meaning, suggesting that she is not old, but immature.

The meaning or emphasis of a given sign is changed by simultaneously altering the behavior of the body. This nonmanual paralanguage feature of ASL is not created on the spot by individual signers, but rather selected from a familiar lexicon of specific expressions known and implemented by all signers.

WORDS OF ASL

For any two languages, one cannot make literal translations from one to the other in a word-for-word fashion. Anyone who has ever tried to translate or interpret will be well aware of this phenomenon. From ASL to English such word-for-word translation is patently impossible. For instance, in English the one word *light*, derives its meaning from its context within a sentence. In ASL, there are three words

for *light*, one meaning "light" as opposed to "heavy," another meaning "light" as opposed to "dark," and the third meaning "light" as
a fixture or lamp used for illumination.

Although this feature of ASL makes direct correspondence with
English unattainable, it provides unique opportunities for referent
assimilation. (This will be addressed in greater depth in Chapters 3
and 10.) Likewise, signs' iconic nature, their ability to make word
pictures in the air, is visible evidence of their delivering word meanings. Of course, space as the medium of ASL transmission invites a
much greater degree of iconicity than is possible in spoken or written
language.

Iconic examples of referent transparency in ASL that readily render
clear word meanings include the signs for *airplane, tree, monkey,
waiter, car*, and *flower*. The sign for *airplane* shows the shape of the
wings, and the sign for *tree* shows the shape of the trunk. Both describe in space what the referent looks like. The sign for *monkey* shows
the monkey scratches itself, and the sign for *waiter* shows the waiter
serves. Both describe in space what the referent does. The sign for
car shows driving a car, and the sign for *flower* shows smelling a
flower. Both describe in space what you do with the referent.

An extension of signs' ability to demonstrate meaning through the
iconic property is their facility in creating a concrete expression of an
abstract referent. The sign for *maybe* is an example of this quality; it
is moving both extended flat hands alternately up and down. It symbolizes the weighing of one thing against another. Conceptualizing
an abstract word's meaning in this way is a significant and singular
attribute of ASL.

MANUAL ALPHABET AND FINGERSPELLING

The American Manual Alphabet is a one-handed configuration of
each of the twenty-six letters of the alphabet. A pictorial representation, virtually identical to the alphabet in use in the United States
today, can be found in an ancient prayer book from the Benedictine
monastery in Cluny, France. This documents the use of these letter
shapes even before the eleventh century. The hand alphabet, as it is
referred to in the early text, is assumed to have its origins in monastic
communities where monks used it to spell various words during their
times of silence and to assist their ministry to the deaf and dying.

Fingerspelling is using the set of handshapes known as the *Ameri-*

can Manual Alphabet to represent letters of English words visually, in just the same way as they can be spelled out orally by naming each of the letters in turn. The sign languages of other countries have their own manual alphabets for the spoken and written languages of those countries. For instance, in the United Kingdom there is a two-handed alphabet that accompanies British Sign Language. This alphabet is quite different from the one in use in the United States, although both are used to spell English words.

When right-handed people are fingerspelling, the handshapes of the manual alphabet are formed by the right hand at a comfortable position in front of the right shoulder. Typically, proper names and technical terms taken from English are fingerspelled. When beginning signers are communicating with a person competent in written English and they do not know the ASL sign for a word, they often resort to fingerspelling.

There are many signs that are referred to as *initialized signs.* These are ASL signs that have borrowed or incorporated the first letter of the corresponding English word. Days of the week are an example of initialized signs, as is the sign formed by moving two hands in outward arcs creating a horizontal circle that means "family" when it is constructed with an *f* handshape, "class" when it is a *c* handshape, and "group" when it is a *g* handshape.

VARIETIES OF ASL

Varieties of ASL are perhaps the most difficult area to write about because they are often misunderstood. Sign language has been used by Deaf people in Deaf communities all over the world for centuries. It is the natural first language for Deaf people. When Deaf people begin their formal education they need to learn written languages. The first written language they are usually taught in school is the predominant language in their own country. In the United States they would learn English. Sign language would be the currency for teaching English. To teach English with sign language you must put the ASL words in English word order, losing the ASL structure and syntax. When this is done the language you have created is an artificial language. Although it serves its function as a teaching tool, it is not a true language.

For instance. Manually Coded English uses the handshapes of the first letter of English words to adapt ASL signs. The original ASL sign for *try* used an *s* handshape. The traditional gesture formed with a *t*, an *a*, or an *e*, respectively, means "try," "attempt," or "effort" in Manually Coded English. These "pidgin" sign language systems have been given various names generally indicating their focus: *Pidgin Signed English* (PSE), *Conceptually Accurate Signed English* (CASE), *English Sign Language* (ESL), *Signing Exact English* (SEE), the *Rochester method*, and *Visual English* are but a few.

These varieties of sign language are used as teaching aids in Deaf education and as the means to communicate between hearing teachers and Deaf students. Hearing family members of Deaf children also rely on these pseudo–sign languages to facilitate family communication and understanding. Until recently, they were also taught to hearing people who wanted to communicate with Deaf friends or coworkers. In the new millennium, with the wider acceptance of ASL, it is more common for schools to offer classes in ASL.

ASL AS A FOREIGN LANGUAGE

When you examine the history of ASL you realize that although it is an old language, which has been used for centuries, from the point of view of many linguists and educators it is a new language. Up until the final third of the twentieth century many educators believed signing was a degenerate form of English, only capable of communicating concrete ideas, little more than pantomime.

This misconception about ASL's status as a language stems in part from confusing speech with language. Speech, like writing or signing, is merely an external form of language. Those who study linguistic structure believe that the part of the brain that deals with the organization of language works independently of the channel through which the language is either produced or perceived. Whether a language is taken in through the ears and sent out through the mouth or in through the eyes and out through the hands, its basic structural properties remain the same.

Although linguistic research has proved conclusively that ASL is a natural language, both linguistically and culturally equivalent to other languages, gaining acceptance of its use in schools to fulfill foreign language requirements has been a struggle. Some of the resistance, of course, is political in nature, for when you accept ASL as a foreign language and students take the ASL courses, there are fewer students remaining to enroll in more traditional foreign language courses such as French, German, or Spanish. This creates a potential problem within academic settings.

During the 1980s and 1990s this situation fostered much discussion on college campuses throughout the United States. In these venues, it was pointed out that although ASL was used by American Deaf people, it was indeed a language different from English. *Foreign* need not have a purely geographic connotation, but could mean "unrelated to" or "unfamiliar to," and surely from that perspective ASL was foreign to most students. In this same vein foreign languages are often studied to break down the barriers between cultures. Learning ASL as a foreign language could help eliminate barriers between Deaf people and English-speaking people. To those who objected that ASL had no written component, it was stressed that less than 10 percent of the languages spoken in the world have a written component. Therefore, a written component cannot logically be a prerequisite of a foreign language.

Another aspect of ASL that was emphasized by its proponents was that it is one of the most commonly used languages in the United States and as such has great career value. ASL/English users are considered bilingual in the job market, and ASL meets the requirements for bilingual pay. For example, doctors and nurses who know ASL become eligible for pay increases.

Since the Americans with Disabilities Act (ADA) passed into law in July 1990, there have been many more employment opportunities for sign language interpreters. As the visual landscape has changed with ramps, altered curbs, and additional elevators providing access as a direct result of the ADA, an equivalent, albeit less apparent response to the same law is mandating sign language interpreters for deaf citizens in all public institutions receiving federal funding. This equal access provision is fostering additional ASL use in the United States.

The upshot of the increase in the need for sign language interpreters is a corresponding increase in the number of people learning ASL as they prepare to fill these new positions. Other college students, not necessarily interested in using ASL in their career endeavors, are taking ASL courses to fulfill liberal studies foreign language requirements, as are an increasing number of younger students who take sign language in high school.

ASL was accepted as a foreign language in all California high schools in 1987. Since that time, many other states and school districts have followed suit. As the twentieth century drew to a close, it was not unusual to find sign language courses in educational institutions. In fact, it is estimated that at any given time over one hundred thousand people are engaged in learning ASL. This figure does not include the young children who learn some sign in their nursery and preschool classes or the adults engaged in sign classes at churches and other social agencies.

CONCLUSION

Sign language has had a long, complicated, interesting history. It is the native language of over one half million individuals in the United States, and, as such, it is seen as a symbol of cultural unity for the Deaf community. Recognized in recent decades by linguists as an authentic language, equivalent to any other language, ASL has taken on new dimensions as a foreign language as its use in educational institutions has increased. There are nearly 15 million people in North America able to communicate to some degree in sign language, making it the third most commonly used language in the country.

_____ Chapter 3 _____

Reading

What exactly is reading? When does reading begin? Do children have to be taught to read? Does reading happen spontaneously for anyone? Is reading a system? When a person is reading, are words and letters identified individually? Because this book is intended for some readers who may not know the answers to these questions, this chapter attempts to put forth a few explanations. As the description of the reading process unfolds, the theoretical implications of how and when sign language could enhance or benefit the endeavor is explored. (This idea is addressed more fully in Chapter 10.)

Reading is the ability to capture the meaning of words without effort in an automatic manner, with enough cognitive energy remaining for the individual reader to move on to comprehension. Reading proficiency is limited by the speed, accuracy, and effortlessness with which readers can respond to print as coherent orthographic, phonological, and semantic (meaning-bearing) patterns. In reading, the process supporting orthographic, phonological, and semantic identification of words occurs interactively and interdependently. Without the complete and proper operation of all three, the reader is left with neither capacity nor support for comprehension.

Reading is a system, whose parts are not discrete, but should grow together and develop conjointly. The lower- and higher-order pieces of the structure are linked by dependent connections between them.

Cognizance of these connections is constantly clarified as the reading system develops in an interrelated procession of reinforcing growth.

We would like children to read well so they might enjoy the pleasure and educational advantage of print. To read well one must read often. Children are induced to read a lot by receiving some reward, excitement, or pleasure from their effort. Providing this inducement becomes a difficult dilemma when you are involved with beginning readers. Maintaining some sort of parity between effort and reward can be a struggle.

Although the instructional principles do not change, some instructional practices are particularly appropriate for young learners. There is a body of literature that indicates a child's familiarity with the letters of the alphabet and speech sounds or phonemes is a strong predictor of the child's future reading capacity. Children who learn the letters and have garnered some phonemic awareness before they enter school have begun to learn to read.

Such findings point toward augmenting and enhancing children's literacy and linguistic experience before they enter school. The child's degree of engagement with and attention to print and individual capacity for reading, its ease or difficulty, depend in large measure on what has transpired before school starts.

Reading depends on knowledge of spelling and of spelling-sound relationships. Acquiring this knowledge and using it depend on the child's interest in the reading process. Heightening a child's interest in learning to read may be the strongest contribution sign language will make to the reading process.

Learning to read a language is not like learning to speak a language. Children all over the world acquire their native language in a natural manner, without any instruction. By the age of five or six, youngsters possess a complete language system with an apparently built-in understanding of its grammar, syntax, and structure. This occurs whether the language is English, French, or even a signed language, such as ASL. The universality of the language-acquisition process suggests that the human species is innately endowed with special language-acquisition abilities, and that language itself is biologically and genetically part of the human neurological system.

There is no such corresponding human proclivity for reading. Young children have no innate understanding of or even a concept of individual letters or individual words in print. They are familiar with listening to words and familiar with saying words, but they need to be taught to be aware of the printed word. When children first listen to a group of spoken words, they hear one long string. Divisions into unique word segments are not discernible. The concept of viewing words as individual whole entities or the one-by-oneness of words is where reading instruction begins.

LEARNING TO READ

Before acquiring the concept that words are discrete entities or concurrently with learning this concept, depending on which reading specialist you follow, children must have a thorough knowledge and understanding of the letters and sounds of the alphabet. There is a progression of learning that begins with the names of the letters. They are often taught from the "Alphabet Song," set to the tune of "Twinkle, Twinkle, Little Star." Most children are able to learn it rather quickly and easily.

It is important to establish the names of the letters before making any attempt to describe their shape or their sound. Knowing the names of the letters first gives children a mnemonic hook where they may hang other aspects of those letters. When children know the letters' names well before they are introduced to their sounds, they are far less likely to be confused when sounds are later introduced. Remember that children are quite young when they are able to distinguish between the name of an animal and the sound the animal makes.

If you are planning to include sign instruction in the learning process, teaching the manual alphabet when you teach the names of the letters is a good idea. Make the letter shapes as you sing or recite the alphabet. Young children will follow and mimic your actions with little prompting as they respond to what, to them, becomes a sort of finger play. Children learn these hand configurations of the manual alphabet quite readily. If there are mistakes they are visually identifiable. The teacher or parent can quietly correct the handshape by molding the child's hand into the correct letter shape or position.

Ideally, after children have learned the names of the letters their written shapes and the sounds of spelling are introduced. This is another step in the process when sign language can enhance the assimilation of knowledge. Customarily at this juncture, each letter's form and sound and a meaningful representative word are conjointly presented, providing an entry for all three processors (orthographic, phonological, semantic) in the reading system. Key word charts often support this function.

These aids depict a visual form of the letter and a picture of a word that typifies the letter's most familiar sound association. For instance, the letter *f* is displayed next to a flower. Providing a prototypical pronunciation of the letter helps to regulate or focus the sound response in the phonological processor at the same time that the key word image becomes a pictorial mnemonic. Such charts are extremely beneficial in the classroom and generally serve their purpose quite well, but it is difficult to take them on the road.

In this instance sign language can assist the reading process by providing a portable key word chart for the letter sounds. In the previous example the letter *f* was coupled with a picture of a flower. If you were using sign language enhancement with your young learner, you would teach the manual sign for *f* and the sign for *flower*. The ASL sign for *flower* suggests holding a flower to the nose to smell it. To make the sign you touch the fingertips of the right flattened *O* hand, palm facing in, to either side of the nose.

When each letter of the alphabet is taught to children in this fashion with an accompanying key sign word that demonstrates the letter's primary sound, emerging readers have a key to unlock the visual motor and phonological properties of letters. Unlike a typical cardboard key word chart that remains in school, the key sign words can accompany children wherever they go and can be used to invoke the sounds of letters. The signs become part of their memory and remain with them over long periods. A number of additional memory stores are activated when sign language is added to the mix. We have a new language to deal with, an augmented visual aspect, and what has been termed *motor memory*. (More information about these aspects can be found in Chapter 9.)

LEARNING TO SPELL

The orthographic processor cannot begin to learn spellings until it has learned to recognize and identify the letters easily. As previously indicated, teaching the names of the letters first, and then their shapes and sounds by association with a key word, is the way to proceed with respect to spelling as well as reading. A carefully chosen key sign word will have an onset and rime (part of the word that follows the onset letter) that can be used later for a word family or phonogram.

The groups *sit, bit, hit; man, pan, can*; and *mat, hat, cat, sat, fat* are good examples. Your key word for *c* would be *cat*, for *p* would be *pan*, for *s* would be *sit*. Learning these key word signs for letters and moving on to incorporate phonograms from them heighten the prospect of spelling success.

You may have noticed that in this method the suggested key word is not always a noun. The iconic aspect of sign language is an inherent attribute that fosters referent transparency; a traditional key word chart would not normally include *sit*, because it is a verb and there is nothing concrete to display on the chart to spur a child's memory.

On the other hand, the sign for *sit* symbolizes a person's sitting and is formed by placing the palm side of the right *H* fingers on the back of the left *H* fingers held in front of the chest, palm facing down, fingers pointing right; then moving both hands down slightly. Teaching this sign as the key word for the letter *s* works quite nicely. Signs' contribution to referent support permits a greater range of word types to be introduced early. Entire simple sentences can be formed with the initial words learned from sign language key word charts.

The next step in the instruction program is teaching the manual alphabet. Rather than confusing children and making them less able to identify the printed form of the letter, learning the manual alphabet appears to help children clarify their thinking and fosters print awareness and recognition. (This idea is not new; more can be found about its historical aspect in Chapter 9.)

The children quickly move on to fingerspelling with the manual alphabet. This is easier and quicker for them than printing the letters. The letters of a word are fingerspelled and spoken at the same time. The sequence begins as the word is displayed in print. The word is spoken and signed, then the letters in the word are simultaneously recited and fingerspelled. Again the word is spoken and signed, completing the training sequence.

Children are also taught, at other times, to print the letters; they are given many opportunities to practice their printing and make clear associations between their efforts and printed words in text. Introduction of fingerspelling before printing is related to children's developmental process. It is important to remember that the fine motor skills necessary for writing and printing take longer to mature and it is far more age-appropriate for children to fingerspell than to print with a pencil on paper. Fingerspelling is also a more effective tool in learning how to spell words and remembering how to spell them.

When a child fingerspells a word, the action is completed more quickly than if the child were laboriously working with a pencil on paper. Refer to the previous example from the sign key word chart using the word *sit*. Think about the difficulty a five- or six-year-old child would have constructing *sit* in print. Those three little letters contain many strokes and movements, as well as an extremely large number of discrete visual concepts in order to place the lines properly. The *s* is half the size of the *t*. The *i* has a dot that seems to be higher than the top of the *t*. Now look at that *t* and consider how hard it is to place that horizontal cross line above the midway point of the vertical line, creating four equal angles were the lines cross each other.

It is much easier to fingerspell *sit* than to print *sit*. All the signs of the manual alphabet are constructed with the palm in a forward position. *S* is a closed fist; *i* is the pinkie up; *t* is the thumb tucked between the first and second fingers.

Studies show that a child's memory of the spelling sequence of words is dramatically improved when he or she is taught spelling with this method. Fingerspelling involves both a thinking activity and a physical activity. The two aspects, joined in tandem, generate a powerful influence on the memory. Familiarity with the sound-symbol structure of words is internalized and retained with a fingerspelling approach.

Complementing these findings, the activity of manually fingerspelling a word reinforces a child's ability to write or read or say it. Feeling a word strengthens existing associations among writing a word, reading a word, and saying a word. Clearly children need solid visual knowledge of letters to read well; when this visual knowledge is overlaid with the feel of the letter, reading becomes easier.

It has additionally been argued that, in general, spelling instruction is critical for reading success for the following reasons: Learning about spelling elaborates and reinforces knowledge in the orthographic processor, and it enhances reading proficiency as spelling knowledge articulates with knowledge in the phonological processor. This brain activity strengthens children's ability not just to induce spellings but to hear and pronounce words correctly in their oral activities.

PERSONAL TEXTS

Personal texts are books that children write about their own experience. This idea harkens back to suggestions from Maria Montessori, who advocated, "Write first, read later." It is a language experience approach that helps convey and refine the relationship between print and language meaning. This writing-to-read technique also lends itself to a new incarnation when it meets with sign language adaptation. Sign is a natural medium for clarifying the referent for the word, and long before a child can construct a story in print, it is possible for a child to convey a story in sign language.

Although at first glance personal sign language "texts" may appear unusual, they teach children several of the key concepts reading instructors are striving to convey. The individual nature of a word is displayed, as each sign represents one word, demonstrating the one-by-oneness of words. The relationship between language and thought is present as children build stories from their own vocabulary of signs. Personal texts created in sign language let children experiment with writing in a unique manner. The stories can be remembered and signed repeatedly, and as the child's printing ability escalates, the stories can be transcribed into print.

Personal texts help children develop a basic understanding of the forms and function of text and its relevance to their own lives. They become more aware of the structure of language: From letter sounds they form words, from words they form sentences, and from sentences they form stories. These insights are gained interactively from a practical personal perspective. The final creative product is a permanent written record of their thoughts and their achievement.

PICTURES

Signs function as pictures. In selecting reading books for children the quality of the pictures is an important factor because these visual images support the text. If sign language constitutes a portion of the reading instruction, the signs actually function as built-in pictures for amplifying the text. They help children understand the meaning of the text by serving as clear referents for the words and the stories that emerge from combining the words. Sign language supplies enticingly attractive comprehension support.

WORDS

What about words? Words have many elements. Spelling, meaning, and pronunciation are connected in a specific learned relation to each other. The energy that any one unit or set of units can pass to any other unit depends on the strength and completeness of the connections between them. The strength and completeness of the connections depend strictly on learning. From a physiological perspective, most children are equipped with well-designed associative architecture that gives them the intellectual wherewithal to learn about relationships among these units.

It may surprise you to learn that even skillful readers and mature adult readers look at every word and individually process letters. Each individual letter activates its own recognition unit in the reader's memory. These directly activated units, in turn, send attention to each other, with the result that the associations between them are strengthened, as the automatic consequence of looking at the word. Readers do skip over the function words like *of, in, to,* and *the,* but research demonstrates there is a relatively complete processing of the words and individual letters of print. Visual processing of each letter does occur even in accomplished readers, and when these competent readers are reading for comprehension they devote even more time to each individual word and process its component letters quite thoroughly.

Meaningful experiences with words are important to the acquisition of their spelling, as well as their usage and interpretation. The visual memory for individual printed letters is based on interrelations of line segments and areas as they appear on the printed page. Visual memories of words help children form spelling patterns. These memories enrich existing orthographic knowledge and build new phonological associations. Reading meaningful words in meaningful contexts will assist children in establishing a useful visual vocabulary.

FINAL THOUGHTS OR BACK WHERE WE STARTED

Throughout this chapter the overwhelming importance of letter recognition to the reading process has been stressed. Young children must be able to recognize individual letters with ease and accuracy before word recognition instruction commences. It is impossible to overstate this simple truth, as individual letters are the key that unlocks the reading system. The more emergent readers are engaged in activities that pay attention to the letter-by-letter structure of words, the more likely they are to become good readers.

Awareness of individual letters and the ease with which they can be identified are indications that the child will become a successful reader for a number of reasons. The speed with which letters are named correctly is an index of the thoroughness of the child's facility in identifying letters. Children with confident knowledge of letter names will have an easier time learning letter sounds.

If a reader gets stuck on one letter, intaking the entire sequence is interrupted. When the child must work on identifying the pattern of an individual letter, they will have less energy to invest in recognizing words. When a child is uncertain about the letters' identity, growth in their visual vocabulary is impeded. A child who automatically and effortlessly sees letters as wholes will see words as patterns of letters.

Both letter names and sounds are indicators of reading potential, and both are critical for the beginning reader. In general, names of letters relate to their sounds. Comfortable knowledge of letter names hastens children's learning of their sounds because it mediates their ability to remember sounds. A child who is sure the symbol *s* represents the letter *s* can use that information to recall the sound of the letter *s*. Conversely, a child who is unsure whether the symbol is the letter *s* or the letter *e* is confused, and no clear referent sound emerges to reveal the word or its sound meaning.

The predictive and correlational power of letter naming speed is that the ability to name any kind of visual stimulus rapidly or automatically reflects a deep capacity that differs between individuals and is important for reading. This hypothesis has grown from findings that good and poor readers tend to differ in the speed with which they can name colors, numbers, and objects.

In essence these good readers evidence fine visual perception characteristics. The next logical step is to train the visual processor. As indicated earlier, adding sign language to reading instruction provides significant opportunity for enhancing children's visual acuity. It is a proactive developmentally appropriate activity engaging children's active attention. It can become an important contributor providing activity and action as it trains the child to focus visually and to attend.

Sign language and its affiliated manual alphabet support can nourish reading instruction. Albeit an additional step, it is a step well worth taking because of the advantages it offers. Children exposed to sign language and the manual alphabet are more readily able to translate letters and words to written language and reading. Because sign initiates a clear image of the letter and its sound and the word and its referent, viewing signs, generating signs, feeling signs, and fingerspelling words, while hearing and seeing print, provide a visual and motor link to the meaning processor.

To reiterate one final time, reading begins with learning the alphabet. You must teach the part as a whole (*ABC*) so the listener will respond to parts as wholes and learn the sequence letter-word-phrase-sentence. Identify letters and link the letters to the sounds, proceed to link the letters to the words, link the words to meanings, and progress to link the words to phrases, and continue the linking process with a complete sentence. Reading is an interrelated process, a linking system.

Before reading instruction begins children must learn to recognize all of the individual letters of the alphabet. They must also be interested in their use. The interest aspect is an important ingredient, decisive in determining a child's facility with print. Including sign language in the reading process can often spark this interest. Finally, reading acquisition is further mediated by perceptual skills, motor skills, spatial relations, perceptual memory, visual memory, visual-motor integration, gross and fine motor coordination, and tactile, kinesthetic activities.

PART II
Research

Chapter 4

My Studies with Typical Students

This chapter recounts chronologically all of the research studies I have directed since 1991 concerning the use of sign language with typical hearing children. The findings have been published in academic journals; the headings of the sections that follow are the titles of the articles that detail those studies and their findings. A brief original abstract follows each title. For readers who would like to consult the articles, they are listed in the References at the end of the chapter. In this summary of those studies, I have attempted to make the language more informal and user-friendly, while providing a comprehensive summary of the research.

ASL AS A FACTOR IN ACQUIRING ENGLISH

This is a study of fourteen hearing children who learned ASL as preschoolers that shows that bimodal, bilingual youngsters achieve significantly higher scores on the Peabody Picture Vocabulary Test than hearing children who know no sign. The scores indicate the positive influence of sign language on a hearing child's acquisition of English.

Background

The impetus for this study, as for many research projects, origi-
nated with anecdotal reports. When I was teaching at Central Connecticut State University in New Britain, Connecticut, students
completing communication degrees reported some interesting observations. They noted that hearing children with parents who were deaf
were demonstrating well-above-average ability in English language
arts. This finding seemed curious because these children were encountering very little English in the home in which they were being
reared.

In this region of Connecticut, with its proximity to the Hartford
School for the Deaf, many baccalaureate degree students have associate degrees as interpreters and work as such. One of the tasks these
young women and men fulfill in their jobs is serving as interpreters
for Deaf parents of hearing children during elementary school parent-
teacher conferences. They reported that the young hearing children,
who know ASL, with whom they interact seemed to have an increased
facility with English and a larger vocabulary than their counterparts
who did not know sign.

At the time this phenomenon was related to me, I had no logical
explanation for it. I became interested in this apparent paradox and
began to read about ASL and make inquiries among people associated
with the Deaf community. A similar message was conveyed to me by
the interpreters working out of the Bergen Community College Program in Paramus, New Jersey. They functioned in much the same
way as the students with interpreters' positions in Connecticut. During parent-teacher conferences they observed that hearing students
who acquired ASL as preschoolers tended to have larger English vocabularies and were doing extremely well in language arts.

I began teaching at Penn State University and maintained my interest in discovering more about the relationship between ASL and English. In the service area for the Scranton State School for the Deaf
in northeastern Pennsylvania where my campus was located, I heard
the same report. Debra Maltese, North East Regional Director for
the Deaf and Hearing Impaired, wondered why many of the interpreters who worked with the local Deaf community noticed in their
roles with hearing children and Deaf parents that the bilingual youngsters were gaining excellent competence in English.

These anecdotal reports from three distinct locations seemed to indicate more than pure coincidence. Did these children, bilingual in English and ASL, actually possess a larger English vocabulary? Would testing such children produce any substantive results? Finding the answers to these questions drove me to design my first research study in this area. I reviewed all of the available literature on this subject before I began. (That literature review and additional studies, conducted since that time by other researchers, can be found in Chapter 6.)

Research Study

In fall 1991 and spring 1992, with the help of Debra Maltese I located fourteen children whose parents consented to their participation in the testing project. The children were all tested on Saturday afternoons at the Scranton State School for the Deaf. This location was selected because they were familiar and comfortable with the surroundings.

The children all had normal hearing. They learned ASL as preschoolers and were fluent in it and in English. With the exception of one child, who was the daughter of an interpreter, they all have one or more Deaf parents. At the time the test was administered they ranged in age from two years ten months to thirteen years six months (see Table 4.1).

Testing Procedure

The assessment instrument chosen for the study is the Peabody Picture Vocabulary Test (PPVT). This well-respected, reliable testing device published by American Guidance Company has been in use since the 1960s in its original form. The 1981 revised version (PPVT-R) employed is an individually administered norm-referenced, wide-range power test of hearing vocabulary. It has been found to be neutral to tester influence. The test is designed for hearing persons two years six months through forty years of age. The PPVT-R was standardized nationally on a carefully selected sample of 5,028 persons (4,200 children and adolescents and 828 adults). Ethnic composition of the norm sample was similar to that of the total U.S. population with 422 African American children represented in the

Table 4.1
PPVT-R Scores

Chronological Age	Gender	Standard Score
3 years 3 months	male	107
2 years 10 months	female	106
9 years 4 months	male	117
7 years 3 months	male	121
3 years 0 months	female	99
5 years 4 months	female	104
6 years 0 months	male	107
7 years 8 months	female	113
12 years 4 months	female	103
3 years 6 months	male	105
13 years 6 months	female	106
6 years 2 months	female	105
7 years 10 months	female	126
11 years 7 months	female	115

sample. In this test raw scores are converted to age-referenced norms or standard scores. The standard testing scores have a mean of 100 and a standard deviation of 15.

The Peabody was administered in the usual fashion with a participant seated at a table or desk with the examiner. The subjects were shown a series (generally thirty-five to forty-five) of test items arranged in order of increasing difficulty. Each item has four simple black-and-white illustrations arranged in a multiple-choice format. The subject's task is to select the picture considered to best illustrate the meaning of a stimulus word presented orally by the examiner. The testing procedure takes about fifteen minutes for each child.

Results

The mean derived score of the fourteen children on the PPVT-R was 109.57 with a standard deviation of 7.38. A one-sample t test indicates that this mean is significantly higher ($p < 0.001$) than the expected value of 100. On such a test an ordinary random sample of subjects would be expected to show variation in scores, but if the sample were large enough, the mean of the scores would be at or close to 100. The testing instrument's norming group of 4,200 children constitutes a control group with a mean of 100. The bilingual, bimodal children who participated in this project achieved scores significantly higher than scores expected from a randomly selected sample. The 109.57 mean score earned by the bilingual, bimodal youngsters is a powerful number that clearly indicates that children who learned ASL as preschoolers acquired a larger English vocabulary than is expected of typical children.

This first research study supported the anecdotal observations of my students from the communication theories class at Central Connecticut State University and inspired my continued interest in the subject. During my examination of the literature pertaining to sign language I had read Oliver Sacks's book *Seeing Voices*. Within this information laden book, he writes in a footnote about a program taking place in Prince George's County, Maryland, in which hearing children were using sign language in typical public school education to improve their English. This is where I conducted my next research.

THE EFFECT OF SIGN LANGUAGE ON HEARING CHILDREN'S LANGUAGE DEVELOPMENT

Students in prekindergarten classes who receive sign instruction test significantly higher on the Peabody Picture Vocabulary Test than students in prekindergarten classes not receiving sign instruction. Their superior scores indicate that simultaneously presenting words visually, kinesthetically, and orally enhances a child's language development.

Background

Following the lead I found in Sacks's *Seeing Voices*, I contacted the Prince George's County supervisor for early childhood education and discovered that this Maryland county had a strong early childhood language focus. They were well aware of the links between language acquisition and educational progress. They knew children with limited language capabilities are disadvantaged learners and were attempting to improve their student's language ability. Because of the large African American population in their county, there were concerns about the studies that show that black children consistently test 15 points lower than white children on standard tests and general agreement with the educators who believe this difference is largely the result of black children's poor mastery of the white middle-class school dialect.

They understood that young learners' language proficiency is critical for communication facility and academic success and were attempting to take advantage of the small window of optimal opportunity that exists during the prekindergarten years for young children to acquire language readily. The program they had designed operates during this accelerated language growth period, which developmentally occurs in early childhood. Although the program had been implemented and appeared effective, they had no funding for assessment. When I approached them and offered to conduct a study, they gladly accepted.

The Prince George's County language intervention procedures form the basis for the research study that is described next. The investigation attempts to discover whether adding sign language to prekindergarten curriculum increases hearing children's receptive English vocabulary. The research was conducted during the late spring of 1992 and reports the results of a bilingual approach with African American children in a prekindergarten program.

In the language intervention procedure two languages are used, English and ASL. ASL is a separate independent language, distinct from the English of its surrounding community. It is complexly structured, exhibiting all the fundamental properties linguists require of any language. (Sign language is analyzed more fully in Chapter 2.) The special form or mode in which ASL's properties are manifested is the visual-gestural mode. Therefore, children in this program have a bilingual (English/ASL), bimodal (voice-aural/gestural-visual) experience.

Research Study

The participants in this study were sixty students in four prekindergarten classes in the Prince George's County, Maryland, early childhood program. The classes were the same size and participants were from two schools in the same district located in adjoining neighborhoods with analogous socioeconomic status. The best indicator of the students' common socioeconomic status is that both schools are classified as Title 1. Under federal regulations, a school has a Title 1 classification when over 50 percent of the students in each class qualify for free lunch. The schools' Title 1 ranking indicated there were no significant differences in parental income. All of the student participants were African American and were in the program for the entire year. The common racial characteristic was the result of happenstance and not design.

Two of the classes tested received sign instruction, as described in the Treatment Procedure section. The other two classes received traditional instruction and were taught no sign. In all other respects, the curriculums for all of the four classes were identical. The same teacher taught both signing classes in one school, and another teacher taught both nonsigning classes in another school. The county supervisor of early childhood education reports that the two white teachers possess similar qualifications and have received excellent teacher evaluations. They both have been in the system ten years. Prior to the ASL intervention, there was virtually no difference in the scores their classes earned on kindergarten placement measures.

Treatment Procedure

In the Prince George's County sign instruction classes, teachers begin the school year using sign language simultaneously with spoken English. They sign words and phrases, not necessarily whole sentences. Signs are introduced to emphasize words and stressed for requests and commands. Examples are *sit, stop, stand, walk,* and *line up.* When teachers tour their rooms during the first school days, they give a sign label for each center (area of the room for specified activity) and sign the activities engaged in at that center.

Children are taught to sign the alphabet as they learn the letters. Whenever a letter is mentioned, its sign is made: "If your name begins with *D* [signed] you may line up." This kind of expression is repeated many times daily. Children pick up the signs for the alphabet quickly.

For lessons and stories the signs are often introduced and taught first. For example:

Teacher: We are going to hear a story about a bird. Let's all make the sign for *bird.*

Children: (They sign *bird.*)

Teacher: This bird likes a very special tree. Let's all make a tree over here.

Children: (They copy the sign and the placement.)

Then the teacher continues the story or the lesson. The children sign the words with the teacher as she tells the story. Throughout the year as these stories and lessons continue and develop variety, the students acquire a constantly increasing number of signs matched with words.

The teacher communicates with the students by using sign and spoken English words simultaneously about half of the time, using English alone about one quarter of the time, and using ASL alone about one quarter of the time. When the students begin to acquire sign language ability, they spontaneously use the language. Initially, they communicate in sign with their teacher. As the days continue, they independently use sign language with each other in their activity centers. They very quickly become able to communicate quite easily in this nonnative language.

The process of introducing sign to the children is an extremely natural one. It is used consistently (in the proportions previously noted) without any particular attention or stress. Sometimes teachers tell students they can talk with their hands or mention that Deaf people use their hands to speak. For the most part, however, as far as the young students know, all teachers instruct this way. There is a special unit on communication in February. During that period, the children are taught more about deafness and about sign as a language.

Testing Procedure

The testing procedure took place during a one-week period in late spring 1992. The revised Peabody Picture Vocabulary Test (PPVT-R) was administered to the four prekindergarten classes to determine the effect of sign instruction on the students' English language acquisition. The tester was blind to the condition (sign-nonsign) of the students. The participants were shown a series of pages, each containing four black-and-white pictures. They were asked to select the picture that best illustrated the meaning of an orally presented word.

Results

The mean scores on the PPVT-R for the morning and afternoon signing classes were 94.6 and 92.3, with standard deviations of 11.8 and 12.0, respectively. The mean scores for the morning and afternoon nonsigning classes were 78.9 and 77.6, with standard deviations of 10.2 and 13.1, respectively. A two-way analysis of variance indicated that the main effect of signing was statistically significant, $F(1, 56) = 22.06$, $p < .001$, and that the main effect of class meeting time and the interaction effect were not statistically significant, $F(1, 56) = .32$, $p = .58$, and $F(1, 56) = .03$, $p = .87$.

The scores from both sign classes were 15 points higher than those from the classes receiving no sign instruction. Sign instruction brought the scores of these African American students close to the score ordinarily expected for white students (that is, 100). Thus the addition of sign language caused a dramatic increase in these students' vocabulary. The size of a child's vocabulary is significant, because knowing a lot of words means knowing a lot of things. In addition, every word in a child's vocabulary acts as the currency for learning more words.

This research substantiated the anecdotal reports from Connecticut and supported my previous findings from the study in Pennsylvania. I was intrigued by the results. They indicated an extremely large student vocabulary gain, and I decided it would be important to test and compare another pair of classes. The following research study evolved from this desire.

WORDS MORE POWERFUL THAN SOUND

In a study of seventy-six hearing children in prekindergarten classes, half received sign instruction and half did not. They were tested on receptive English vocabulary acquisition. The children receiving sign instruction scored significantly higher on the PPVT-R than those receiving no sign instruction. The results support the hypothesis that hearing prekindergarten children who learn ASL signs improve their acquisition of English vocabulary to a statistically significant degree.

Background

The first research study in Maryland had shown such a dramatic increase in the students' vocabulary that I was heartened by it but also, quite frankly, a bit concerned. Perhaps it was just an anomaly and all of the students with large vocabularies had been placed in one class, and the other class contained all the students with small vocabularies. This did not seem likely, but it was indeed a possibility. I decided it was very important to conduct more research, this time using a pretest and posttest design. The study that is described next attempts to reduce confounding variables by measuring the size of each child's vocabulary gain during the prekindergarten year. It asks, Does adding sign language to prekindergarten curriculum increase hearing children's receptive English vocabulary?

Research Study

The research was conducted with four prekindergarten classes of the same size in Prince George's County, Maryland. The subjects for the study were in two schools in the same school district located in adjoining neighborhoods of comparable socioeconomic status. As in the previous study, the indicator of the students' common socioeconomic status is that both schools have a Title 1 classification, which demonstrates that the students are members of homes with similar household income.

Each of the four classes contained nineteen students. Some moved during the course of the year, but with the addition of new students the class size remained consistent. All the children in the study were black, with the exception of one white child. However, the research project was planned to test the effect of the use of signs, not racial difference.

The students were taught by two teachers, deemed master teachers by their supervisor. Before the ASL intervention began, scores earned at year's end on kindergarten placement measures by the students of both teachers were not significantly different. One teacher taught both signing classes; the other teacher, both nonsigning classes. Each classroom teacher worked with a competent full-time aide. The teachers were both white, the aides both black.

Two of the classes received sign instruction as described in the Treatment Procedure section. The other two classes received traditional instruction with a limited amount of sign. This limited signing took the form of some gestures during story time. In all other aspects, the same curriculum was used for all four classes.

Testing Procedure

To measure the effect of this sign language instruction in relation to the usual prekindergarten program the PPVT-R was again selected. During the first week of school, in September 1992, a tester attempted to pretest all of the students in the four classes with the

PPVT-R, Form M. As in the previously described study, the tester was blind to the condition (sign-nonsign) of the students. It was impossible to test some children because they were absent, a basal could not be achieved, or they were afraid to be tested. (The tester knew the fearful reaction was normal for three- and four-year-old children who had just started school and made no attempt to persuade the young students to be tested.)

At the end of the school year, in the third week of May 1993, all the students previously tested who were still in the program were retested with the PPVT-R, Form L. During both assessment sessions the participants were shown a series of test plates arranged in order of increasing difficulty. Each plate has four simple black-and-white illustrations arranged in a multiple-choice format. The subject's task is to select the picture considered to best illustrate the meaning of an orally presented stimulus word.

Results

The morning nonsign class earned a mean pretest score of 78.08; the afternoon nonsign class earned a mean pretest score of 78.33. The morning sign class earned a mean pretest score of 78.92; the afternoon sign class earned a mean pretest score of 78.33. Because there was no appreciable difference between the morning and afternoon pretest scores in both conditions, and the statistical analysis from the first Maryland study had shown that the effect of class meeting time was not significant, the data from the morning and afternoon classes were combined to give a single mean for both sign classes and a single mean for both nonsign classes.

For the children receiving sign instruction the mean pretest score was 79.03 (standard deviation [sd], 9.7) and mean posttest score 96.27 (sd, 11.61). The corresponding scores for the children not receiving sign instruction were 78.63 (sd, 14.48) and 85.11 (sd, 13.09). Figure 4.1 shows the mean pretest and posttest scores for the children in the signing (S) and nonsigning (N) classes.

A 2 × 2 repeated measures analysis of variance (ANOVA) (Table 4.2) indicated that although the main effect of signing showed a strong tendency, it was not statistically significant $F(1, 47) = 3.55$, $p = .066$. In contrast, the pretest-posttest effect was significant $F(1, 47) = 47.38$, $p = .000$, as was the interaction effect $F(1, 47) = 9.76$, $p = .003$.

Figure 4.1
Pretest and Posttest Scores on PPVT-R

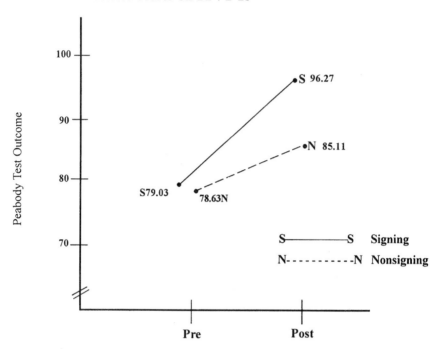

The significant interaction effect clearly indicates differences in the signing and nonsigning conditions on the fall pretest and spring posttest scores. Two independent t tests indicate that the difference between the fall scores for the signing and nonsigning groups was not significant, $t(47) = .116$, $p = .908$, and that the difference between the spring scores for the signing and nonsigning groups was statistically significant $t(47) = 3.12$, $p = .003$.

The pretest or fall scores for the sign and nonsign classes were virtually identical. All of the prekindergarten classes had the same level of competence with receptive English language vocabulary prior to the sign language intervention. When the posttest or spring scores are examined, a dramatic change in the level of competence with receptive English language vocabulary is seen in the students who received sign language instruction. The addition of sign language instruction in their prekindergarten curriculum yielded a striking 17.24 increase in the score that reflects these students' language abilities.

Table 4.2
Summary Anova

Source	SS	df	MS	F	P
Between Subjects					
Signing	777.68	1	777.68	3.55	.066
Error	10281.99	47	218.77		
Within Subjects					
Fall/Spring	3268.91	1	3268.91	47.38	.000
Interaction	673.36	1	673.36	9.76	.003
Error	3243.05	47	69.00		
Total	18244.99	97			

This compares with a 6.48 increase with normal curriculum. Thus the results of this study show a statistically significant improvement in receptive English vocabulary for students who received the sign language instruction.

The African American program participants in this study and in the previous study achieved dramatic language gains, ranging from 15 to 17 points on the PPVT-R. The superior vocabulary scores placed these African American students at the score ordinarily expected for Caucasian students on this measure (100). The statistically significant improvement in English vocabulary demonstrated by the youngsters who were taught sign is a powerful indicator of the value of sign language instruction for hearing prekindergarten students.

This research continued to confirm and support my previous findings concerning sign language and vocabulary growth. However, a number of points continued to concern me: First, I believed that future investigations should attempt to eliminate a confounding element found in this research. If possible, such studies should use the same teacher to teach a signing class and a nonsigning class.

Second, the question of decay over time should be addressed. Would the children maintain the vocabulary growth they acquired during their prekindergarten year during their kindergarten year of school? It would seem from studies of hearing children of Deaf parents that the vocabulary gains would not be lost over time. But on the other hand, there are ample reports that the academic advantages gained by students in head-start programs quickly dissipate and are ultimately lost. The aspect of memory decay over time should be studied.

Third, an interesting spontaneous event was occurring at the time. The teacher who had been the control teacher for my first study in Maryland now wanted to use sign with her students. When she had learned the results of that initial research, showing her students' vocabulary gains were appreciably less than the vocabulary gains achieved by the students in the treatment class, the teacher was both surprised and disappointed by her students' poor outcome. This motivated her to incorporate sign language in her prekindergarten curriculum.

Her interest and action provided a good opportunity to discover more about the process of sign language inclusion from the perspective of the teacher. I decided to track this teacher's students' receptive English vocabulary over a period of years, with a number of classes, to determine whether a relationship existed between students' outcomes and the teacher's signing ability. This investigation became my next research study.

TEACHER ENRICHMENT OF PREKINDERGARTEN CURRICULUM WITH SIGN LANGUAGE

The investigation tracked one prekindergarten teacher's experience over a three-year period to determine whether a relationship exists between student outcomes and a teacher's signing ability. The students' receptive English vocabulary gains indicate a corresponding increase in the teacher's mastery of sign language instruction technique. The study shows that enriching preschool curriculum with sign language ultimately improves hearing African American children's receptive English vocabulary. These findings confirm and extend those of previous research demonstrating that simultaneously presenting words visually, kinesthetically, and orally offers an advantage to young learners. Additionally, it presents an account of the process of prekindergarten preparation, assesses mastery of the teacher's sign language technique in curriculum delivery, examines the manner in which sign language is introduced in the classroom, and explores the theoretical rationale for the student's vocabulary gains.

Background

In the previously cited studies the teachers knew sign language and delivered sign instruction with ease. Their facility with sign language was a given and was not measured. The present study differs from the earlier studies by focusing on the teacher's ability to deliver instruction in sign and incorporate sign language in preschool curriculum. I had not yet investigated this aspect of the treatment procedure. The study was designed to discover whether there is a relationship between student outcomes and a teacher's signing competence. The students' scores on a receptive English vocabulary test are the measure used to determine the teacher's mastery of sign language technique.

Research Study

The teacher subject in this research was the control teacher in one of my earlier sign language projects. During that study she neither knew nor used sign language. She took sign language training and incorporated sign language in her instruction at the start of this study. Her experience is tracked over a three-year period.

The student subjects for this project were 108 prekindergarteners in the Prince George's County, Maryland, early childhood education program. There were 104 African American, 1 white, and 3 Asian children. For each of the three years all students were evaluated with the SHIP readiness screening test prior to the start of classes. On the basis of this instrument they were considered typically developing children, with no disabilities. All of the six classes averaged a similar medium-high rating on the language portion of the SHIP, according to Judy Hoyer, County Director of Early Childhood Education. The six classes varied slightly in size. In the first year, 1993, each class contained nineteen students. In the second year, 1994, each class contained eighteen students. In the third year, 1995, each contained seventeen students.

Treatment Procedure

The teacher prepared by learning sign language from classroom instruction, videotapes, and books. She participated in practice sessions with colleagues who used sign language with their students. She reviewed experienced teachers' lesson plans and discussed the sign intervention process with them.

The teacher modeled her use of sign in classroom management and curriculum delivery on the practices of the other teachers in the early childhood program who were using sign language instruction with their students. (A full description of these activities and actions can be found in the Treatment Procedure section in the discussion of the study, The Effect of Sign Language on Hearing Children's Language Development.) In summary, she began the school year using ASL signs in English word order accompanied by spoken English for single words and short phrases. Signs introduced students to significant words in the curriculum and were used to stress the requests and commands of classroom management.

In addition, children were taught to fingerspell the alphabet as they learned the letters. Whenever a letter was mentioned, its sign was made. They also learned a sign word illustrating the predominant sound with which the letter was associated. For example, the sign for *fly* is introduced when teaching the letter *F*.

The amount of time devoted to signing and using the manual alphabet gradually increased throughout each school year in the same manner and at the same pace. The treatment procedure was employed with one morning and one afternoon prekindergarten class for three successive academic years. Six classes received the sign language treatment.

Testing Procedure

The Peabody Picture Vocabulary Test, 1981 revised version (PPVT-R), was used to assess receptive English vocabulary. (Refer to the full description of the PPVT-R earlier in the chapter.) To measure the effect of the sign language treatment relative to the students' English vocabulary gains the PPVT-R, Form L, was administered as a pretest during the first week of school in September. At the end of the school year, during the third week of May, all those previously tested were retested with the PPVT-R, Form L, to determine the extent of their vocabulary gain.

The PPVT-R was administered and scored in the conventional fashion. The standard score equivalent was calculated for each child. The age-referenced aspect of the PPVT-R takes into account normal vo-

Table 4.3
Pretest and Posttest Scores on PPVT-R

	Pretest	Posttest
1st year	79.03 (sd, 9.7)	85.11 (sd, 13.09)
2nd year	78.63 (sd, 14.48)	88.1 (sd, 13.55)
3rd year	78.9 (sd, 10.2)	98.6 (sd, 13.21)

cabulary gain (that is, a child of five is expected to have a larger vocabulary than a child of four).

The pretest-posttest procedure was repeated in the same sequence with the morning and afternoon classes during each of the three successive years of the treatment program. The increase in students' receptive English vocabulary gains over the three years of classes was used to assess the teacher's mastery of sign language technique.

Results

No significant difference was found between the morning and afternoon children's test scores on the Peabody. Therefore, data were collapsed into one figure representing a single mean for both morning and afternoon pretest scores and a second figure representing a single mean for morning and afternoon posttest scores (Table 4.3 shows the mean for each year).

In 1993, the first year with sign language enrichment, the teacher's students earned the mean pretest score of 79.03 (sd, 9.7), and the mean posttest score of 85.11 (sd, 13.09) on the PPVT-R. A paired t test showed a significant difference between pretest and posttest scores (t, df 18 $= -2.08$; p $< .05$).

In 1994, the second year with sign language enrichment, the teacher's students earned the mean pretest score of 78.63 (sd, 14.48) and the mean posttest score of 88.1 (sd, 13.55) on the PPVT-R. A paired t test showed a significant difference between pretest and posttest scores (t, df 16 $= -9.51$; $p < .001$).

In 1995, the third year with sign language enrichment, the teacher's students earned the mean pretest score of 78.9 (sd, 10.2) and the mean posttest score of 98.6 (sd, 13.21) on the PPVT-R. A paired t test showed a significant difference between pretest and posttest scores (t, df 17 $= -8.55$; $p < .001$).

Analysis of variance tests that compared the scores of the three groups at pretest and posttest periods showed no significant difference between the groups in fall ($F\,2$, $51 = .010$), but a significant difference between the groups in spring ($F\,2$, $51 = 9.79$; $p < .01$), with the year 2 and year 3 scores higher than year 1 scores and the year 3 scores higher than year 2 scores. Table 4.3 shows the means and standard deviations for each year.

After the teacher had gained one year of signing experience her students' scores increased only 6.8 points, with two years of signing experience the scores increased 9.47 points, and with three years of signing experience the scores increased 19.70 points. In order to describe the relationship between the teacher's years of signing experience and the magnitude of the test score increase, the SYSAT software program was used to calculate a Pearson correlation coefficient. A strong positive correlation of $r = .960$ was found. Because of the relatively small number of years involved, this r value was not statistically significant, although it showed a trend toward significance (t, $d\,f1 = p < .09$).

This study adds support to the documented evidence of positive effects of enriching preschool curriculum with sign language. That is, the sign language treatment shows a trend toward improvement in students' receptive English vocabulary, in a direction similar to that reported in earlier research studies.

The fact that all groups of students began the school year with nearly comparable mean pretest scores but concluded each year, as the study progressed over the ensuing years, with increasingly higher posttest scores is likely related to a corresponding increase in the teacher's mastery of sign language technique. Over the three years the program was tracked, student posttest scores escalated steadily, although pretest scores were similar (Figure 4.2).

The students' scores on the PPVT-R improved in a manner consistent with the teacher's years of signing experience. These results suggest that a relationship exists between student outcomes and a teacher's signing competence. As the teacher's comfort and expertise increased there was a parallel increase in her students' scores.

This study represents one teacher's accelerating success with enriching six preschool classes' curriculum with sign language. It offers tentative confirmation for the general hypothesis that when using sign language as an intervention to achieve increased English vocabulary

Figure 4.2
Student Receptive Vocabulary Gains Over Three-Year Period

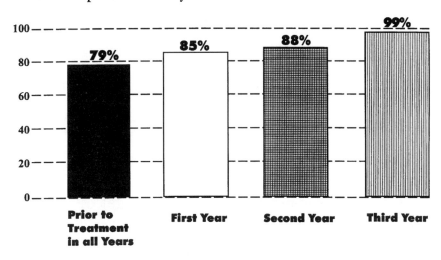

in preschool students, the advantage sign language provides begins when the treatment begins and escalates as the teacher gains experience with sign language.

The teacher's gradual increase in the use of sign language was an asset to her teaching technique, as evidenced by her student's consistently improving receptive English vocabulary scores. The modality change presented no problems for the teacher, who was able to adapt her teaching style steadily to accommodate the new language. According to the teacher, achieving a comfort level in rendering instruction proved to be an uncomplicated natural process.

Specifically, this investigation, which tracked one teacher's experience over three years, clearly indicates the process of enriching prekindergarten curriculum with sign language improves hearing African American children's receptive English vocabulary to a statistically significant degree. The progression in the students' vocabulary gains occurred in a way congruent with the teacher's corresponding mastery of sign language delivery. This suggests that when teachers use sign language as an accompaniment to typical prekindergarten curriculum, the intervention becomes increasingly successful as the teacher gains sign language experience.

The present study's findings confirm and extend those of previous research that demonstrate that simultaneously presenting language in visual, kinesic, and oral ways enhances a young child's English vocabulary development. Furthermore, it presents an account of the process of prekindergarten teacher preparation, assesses a teacher's mastery of the sign language technique in curriculum delivery, and demonstrates the relationship between a teacher's experience and expertise with sign language and a student's receptive English vocabulary gains.

This research had satisfactorily answered one of my previous questions concerning the relationship between student outcomes and teacher ability. A number of concerns remained: Namely, I still wanted to set up a study in which the same teacher would teach both the signing class and the nonsigning class. The question of decay over time continued to concern me; I believed it was important to discover whether the vocabulary gains the students had achieved would be retained. Discovering the answer to this query became the subject of my next study.

SEEING LANGUAGE: THE EFFECT OVER TIME OF SIGN LANGUAGE ON VOCABULARY DEVELOPMENT IN EARLY CHILDHOOD EDUCATION

The study examines the effect over time of the use of sign language in young hearing children's language development. It tests and tracks a class from their first week of school as prekindergarten students over the two-year period that ends with the last week of their kindergarten year. The results indicate that the statistically significant vocabulary gains made in their prekindergarten year are sustained throughout their kindergarten year and remain with them. There is no memory decay over time. These findings strengthen the rationale for including sign language instruction in early childhood education.

Background

The children receiving sign instruction in their prekindergarten classes were demonstrating large advances in their receptive English vocabulary. Unfortunately, the sign instruction was not part of the kindergarten curriculum, so they would be receiving no additional reinforcement. I was concerned about what was happening to their vocabularies during their kindergarten year. Would the impressive vocabulary gains they had achieved disappear by the time they left kindergarten?

In this follow-up study designed to discover the answer to the question, the Maryland students who received the sign language instruction during their prekindergarten year are evaluated with the PPVT-R on a series of different items (Form M) at the end of their kindergarten year to determine whether they have maintained the vocabulary gains of their prekindergarten year. It was hypothesized that there would be no decay over time.

Research Study

The participants in this study were nineteen African American kindergarten students in Prince George's County, Maryland, who had been part of the early childhood program cohort receiving sign instruction in prekindergarten. Eleven of the thirty students constituting the prekindergarten sign classes were no longer in the school system. The nineteen remaining students adequately represent the original group. These students' mean score on the PPVT of receptive English vocabulary on entering school was 77.84 (sd, 9.97), and their mean score at the end of their prekindergarten year was 95.11 (sd, 10.57), showing a 17.27 increase in the score that measures their vocabulary. These statistics mirror the results for the entire original group, who had a pretest mean of 79.03 (sd, 9.7), a posttest mean of 96.27 (sd, 11.61), and a 17.24 increase in the score measuring vocabulary.

Testing Procedure

The assessment instrument was the PPVT-R. The kindergarten students who had received sign instruction in prekindergarten were tested at the end of kindergarten. Their sign instruction was limited to prekindergarten. During their kindergarten year they received no additional sign instruction, nor was the sign they had been taught utilized. Their kindergarten teacher knew no sign and used none.

The testing procedure took place during a one-week period in May 1994. The PPVT-R, Form M, was administered, in the conventional manner, to the nineteen kindergarten students who had taken part in the prior prekindergarten sign instruction intervention to deter-

Table 4.4
PPVT-R Scores for Individual Students

	September Pre-K	May Pre-K	May Kindergarten
Student A	71	110	75
Student B	77	86	88
Student C	83	97	101
Student D	74	66	76
Student E	84	109	101
Student F	93	98	112
Student G	66	82	93
Student H	66	90	74
Student I	89	89	88
Student J	62	97	88
Student K	81	92	92
Student L	89	104	100
Student M	69	90	97
Student N	74	88	96
Student O	72	94	101
Student P	83	99	97
Student Q	96	106	121
Student R	86	109	96
Student S	64	101	96
Cohort Mean	77.84	95.11	94.32
Standard Deviation	9.97	10.57	11.38

mine the effect over time of the prekindergarten year of sign instruction on these students' English vocabulary acquisition.

Results

The mean score earned by the nineteen kindergarten students on the test was 94.32 (sd, 11.38). Their mean score at the end of their prekindergarten year had been 95.11 (sd, 10.57). The difference between these scores is not statistically significant.

These results (Table 4.4) show that the extraordinary 17-point gain in receptive English vocabulary these children had achieved during their sign language–enhanced prekindergarten year continued throughout their kindergarten year. Their vocabulary scores confirm that there was no decay over time and that the benefit resulting from the signing treatment had been maintained.

The age- and grade-referenced nature of the Peabody allows and accounts for anticipated vocabulary growth. These students did have larger receptive English vocabularies than when they were tested at the end of their prekindergarten year. Their raw scores are converted and expressed as derived scores. Derived scores allow an individual's score to be compared with those of a large group of persons of the same chronological age in the same grade, on whom the PPVT-R was standardized.

The addition of sign language instruction in their prekindergarten curriculum produced a dramatic increase in these students' vocabulary. The improvement occurred during the time of the sign intervention and was maintained throughout the kindergarten year that followed. Students' vocabulary growth was sustained in the absence of any further sign instruction or use of sign language within their kindergarten program.

The results of this follow-up research study demonstrate that the vocabulary advancement made by these children as prekindergarten students was maintained throughout their kindergarten experience, in the absence of any additional sign instruction. Furthermore, the latest student scores on the PPVT-R demonstrate there was no memory decay over time, a powerful indicator of the value of sign language instruction for early childhood education.

Although all of my research continued to indicate that sign language gave hearing children an advantage in their acquisition of English vocabulary, I remained interested in conducting a study in which the same teacher would deliver instruction with both sign and nonsign methods. Locating a teacher who would be willing to undertake this project was proving to be exceedingly difficult.

It seems that after teachers use sign language with their students they are extremely reluctant to return to traditional instruction, even for the sake of scientific inquiry. I searched long and hard to find a teacher who would be willing to undertake this research project. Eventually, I was able to locate a kindergarten teacher in a neighboring county who was willing to teach one class with sign and one class without sign.

BILINGUAL, BIMODAL EDUCATION FOR
HEARING KINDERGARTEN STUDENTS

The investigation provides evidence that seventeen students in a kindergarten class who received sign language instruction tested significantly higher on the PPVT-R than seventeen students in a kindergarten class not receiving sign language instruction. The same teacher taught both classes in the experimental program. The study's findings confirm and extend those of previous research that demonstrated that simultaneously presenting words visually, kinesthetically, and orally offers an advantage to young learners.

Background

In all of my studies concerning sign use with hearing children two different teachers had been involved. One teacher would teach the class receiving sign language instruction and the other would teach the class not receiving sign language. In the current research design, the same teacher provides all of the instruction for the sign language class, as well as the instruction for the traditional control class. Identical curriculum is taught in the same school, in the same room, on the same day, by the same teacher.

The kindergarten teacher who agreed to become part of this study taught in Baltimore County, Maryland. In Baltimore County when sign language was used with hearing students it was generally not in the early childhood education program, as it had been in Prince George's County, where my previous sign studies with prekindergarten students had been conducted. The countywide focus, in this adjacent county, was on using sign language in the primary grades to augment the reading and spelling program. However, a transitional period had begun, and sign use was gradually filtering down to the younger grades, as more and more prekindergarten and kindergarten teachers began to include it in their curriculum. The teacher who participated in this project was using sign language in her instruction for the first time.

Research Study

The participants in this study were thirty-four typical (no special needs) white kindergarten students from the middle socioeconomic stratum in two kindergarten classes in Baltimore County, Maryland. The classes contained twenty-two students each, of whom seventeen individuals in each class had parental approval to participate in the testing. All of the elementary school children remained in the program for the entire academic year.

One of the classes tested received sign language instruction, as described previously. The other class received traditional instruction and was taught no sign. In all other respects the curriculum was identical for the treatment class and the control class. The various units of study were taught by the same teacher on the same day to both the experimental signing class and the control nonsigning class. All instruction took place in the same school room during morning and afternoon sessions. Time of day is not considered a factor, as previous research has determined there is no appreciable difference in academic performance between morning and afternoon kindergarten classes.

The teacher providing instruction for this study had more than twenty years of experience teaching kindergarten children in public schools. She initiated the Early Childhood Learning Center at Essex Community College and in addition to her work in the classroom, serves as an adjunct professor at Harford Community College.

Before her involvement with this undertaking she knew no sign language and had never used any in her kindergarten instruction. Her preparation for the research project was similar to the previously described preparation engaged in by the prekindergarten teachers in Prince George's County. She conferred with colleagues who used sign with their early childhood students, viewed videotapes, studied instructional sign books, and learned to sign the vocabulary words needed for the curriculum. The teacher's learning procedures continued throughout the school year, as she attempted to stay at least a week ahead of the students with her new sign vocabulary.

Treatment Procedure

Identical curriculum was used for the treatment class and the control class. The various units of study were covered in each class by the same teacher on the same day in the same classroom. The single pedagogical difference was that the control class received a traditional education without any sign language instruction; the treatment class received a traditional education with sign language instruction.

Before initiating the treatment program the students in the kindergarten class designated for sign instruction were told they would be using sign language in school. This information generated excitement and interest. They were eager to share any words they already knew from television, preschool, or older siblings.

During the first days of the bilingual, bimodal program students in the treatment class were taught and learned to respond to the signs for the compendium of directions that would be used in the classroom on a daily basis. These included, but were not limited to, the signs for *sit, stand, form a circle, quiet, wash your hands, use the toilet, snack time, play time, line up,* and *clean up.*

The children learned to count first and were taught to fingerspell letters of the alphabet as they were introduced with segments of study. Vocabulary words were constantly added in a systematic manner with each new unit. The teacher created a card for each vocabulary word that included the printed word and a picture of the sign for the word. These cards were used in the classroom. For out-of-school practice, the students took home a list of vocabulary words with accompanying sign instructions in the weekly newsletter prepared for the parents.

During the early days of the program the teacher's signs were supported with spoken English. This gradually was eliminated and sign language silently stood on its own. ASL signs were initially presented in English word order. However, throughout the year, as more vocabulary was acquired, a consistent effort was maintained to move to ASL syntax. The difference between English and ASL syntax was explained to the children.

The classroom had a small assortment of books on sign language in the reading center. These became very popular with the students. There was a sign language dictionary in the center, and the pupils often wanted to learn the sign for a word that had not been introduced in the curriculum. At such times, the teacher consulted the easily accessible classroom dictionary while the interested children excitedly waited to learn the new sign. The students rarely forgot a sign and were often able to remember the sign for words more easily than the teacher. If either or both student and teacher forgot a sign for a word they would look it up in the sign dictionary.

Testing Procedure

The initial testing procedure took place during the first week of school in September 1994. At that time, all thirty-four student participants in both classes were tested with the PPVT-R, Form M. This pretest measured all the young participants' vocabulary level before sign intervention. The tester was blind to the condition (sign-nonsign) of the subjects and the Peabody was administered and scored in the conventional fashion.

After the sign language experiment, in spring 1995 all the students were tested again with the PPVT-R, this time using Form L. The standard score equivalent was calculated for each child for the pretest and posttest. The age-referenced aspect of the PPVT-R takes into account normal vocabulary gain (a child of five is expected to have a larger vocabulary than a child of four). This pretest-posttest design served to establish a causal link between the signing treatment and vocabulary growth.

Results

There were seventeen students in each class. This number remained stable throughout the sign intervention process. The nonsign control class earned a mean pretest score of 97.4 on the PPVT-R, Form M. The sign treatment class earned a mean pretest score of 98.6 on the PPVT-R, Form M. The nonsign control class earned a mean posttest score of 105.0 on the PPVT-R, Form L. The sign treatment class earned a mean posttest score of 114.4. The mean gain score earned by the sign class was 15.76, as compared to a mean gain score of 7.0 by the nonsign class. The results show that the sign treatment class had greater English vocabulary gains than the nonsign class. There was a statistically significant difference between the posttest scores of the sign treatment class and those of the control class.

This research, which carefully matched two classes, demonstrates the advantage sign language gives for young hearing students in their acquisition of English vocabulary. However, the advances these white students made were not as large as those earned by the African American students of lower socioeconomic status in my previous studies. It may be that sign provides greater or larger vocabulary gains for students who have greater needs.

Another possible reason the student vocabulary gains in this study were not quite as great as the gains made by the students in the previous studies is that the duration of treatment was shorter. In all of the earlier studies the pretest was given during the first two weeks of school in September and the posttest was given during the last two weeks of May. In this study the pretest was given at the usual time in September, but the posttest was given during March; therefore, the sign treatment was measured over a shorter span of time.

The posttest timing changed because after the spring vacation all of the kindergarten students, both morning and afternoon class, received the sign treatment. This modification of the research design occurred in response to parents' requests. When the parents of the students in the control class, who were receiving no sign language instruction, learned that the treatment class was receiving sign language instruction, they wanted their children also to receive sign language instruction. In an effort to appease these parents, the study was cut short and all students in the kindergarten class received the same education.

This event brings up a difficult aspect of conducting research in public schools. Because parents and teachers are actively involved in the educational process, human emotions often come into play. For example, from the point of view of pure research in some instances it might be better to have a study extend over a longer period. Many times this is just not possible, as parents perceive that the students in the treatment class are receiving an advantage and they demand their child receive equal treatment. This kind of parental pressure occurred in the Baltimore County study.

In my studies with prekindergarten children in Prince George's County, the research design would have been better if both the control class and the treatment class were in the same school. This did not happen because the county director of early childhood education would not pit one teacher against another in the same school. She explained this would be uncomfortable for the teachers, even though the study would compare curriculums and modes of delivery, not teachers. For obvious reasons, within a single school setting, control and treatment classes appear to be in competition; this situation is not something many schools would support.

The feelings and rights of parents, teachers, and students must all be considered when research is attempted in public schools. Accommodating the needs of these various contingencies is an ongoing challenge for researchers. Permission slips are needed for participation in the study and for testing. The students' anonymity must be maintained and carefully protected. No matter how significant the potential research findings may appear, it is important that the research itself not disrupt the equilibrium or ethos of the class or school.

When the results of the study described in this section are reviewed, it is unclear why there was less difference in the students' gain scores, unknown whether the teacher's increased experience with sign language would provide an educational advantage for her students, and unreported what effect the sign language treatment had in the students' home. To find some answers to these queries I decided to conduct an additional study the following year with the same teacher in the same school. The study described next examines these heretofore unexplored areas.

SIGN EDUCATION WITH YOUNG HEARING CHILDREN

The information collected should be beneficial to practitioners who are considering second-language learning or ways to enlarge students' vocabulary, communication skills, or verbal abilities. Five published studies indicate that incorporating ASL in early childhood education improves the receptive English vocabulary of typical young hearing learners to a statistically significant degree. The investigations' specific finding that a kindergarten teacher's increased experience with ASL has no notable effect on student outcomes supports the notion that a minimal amount of preparation will provide a teacher with the medium to effectively incorporate this second language in kindergarten instruction. The research design features a Sign Survey Questionnaire, prepared for the students' primary care givers, which determined whether ASL instruction was an effective communication component between home and school, precipitated participation in the out-of-school setting, engendered positive parental beliefs and behavior, changed student attitudes and outcomes, and provided ancillary social and educational benefits.

Background

The current project is closely related to my previous research but has a different focus and examines two new areas. First, the present research considers the effect of the teacher's ability to deliver instruction in ASL. It was designed to determine whether a teacher's increased experience with signing would translate into greater student vocabulary gains. It was hypothesized that as the teacher's experience and presumed comfort with ASL delivery grew there would be a corresponding increase in their vocabulary. The students' scores on a receptive English vocabulary test are the measure used to determine their vocabulary. It was anticipated that students' posttest scores would be higher the second year the teacher used ASL in the curriculum.

Second, since ASL has been used in Maryland, teachers have consistently reported that sign tends to precipitate participation in the children's education by members of the children's household. This study incorporates a questionnaire, prepared for the student's primary care givers, designed to determine the reaction to the sign intervention in the out-of-school-setting. This tactic would garner data to assess parental beliefs and behavior and discover whether the sign intervention did have an extended impact and could reasonably be considered an effective communication component between home and school.

Research Study

The teacher in this study has over twenty years of experience teaching kindergarten children. She is the teacher who taught both the sign and nonsign classes in the previously described ASL research in Baltimore County, Maryland. Before her preparation for that project she knew no ASL and had never used any in her kindergarten instruction. During that project, referred to as *Year I* in this study, the teacher incorporated ASL in her instruction of students for the first time. In the present study, referred to as *Year II*, conducted the following year, the teacher incorporated ASL in her instruction for the second time. The amount of time devoted to ASL instruction and the curriculum material covered in ASL were the same in Year I and Year II.

The student subjects for the study were fifty-one typical white students from the middle socioeconomic strata, constituting three kindergarten classes. One class was the treatment class from the first year the teacher used ASL, referred to as *Year I*. The other two classes were the morning and afternoon classes from the second year the teacher used ASL, referred to as *Year II*. There were seventeen students in each class and subjects remained in their respective programs for an entire academic year.

Treatment Procedures

The treatment procedures the teacher had used during Year I with only one class were replicated during Year II with both the morning and the afternoon kindergarten class. (A full description of these procedures was given earlier.) In summary, she began using ASL on the first day of school, stressing ASL phrases for requests and commands, such as *come here, pay attention*, and *sit down*. Specific words and phrases were signed in ASL, not whole English sentences. There was never an attempt to sign exact English (SEE) or use Pidgin Signed English (PSE), and an effort to use ASL syntax was maintained.

During opening exercises, signs for the month, the day, and the weather were taught. Students were shown a sign label for each of the activity centers and signs for the activities engaged in at that location. For nouns and verbs featured in lessons and stories, students learned the signs before they saw or heard the stories. ASL signs were regularly used for colors, numbers, and feeling words (*mad, sad, glad*, and so on).

Similarly, children were taught to fingerspell the alphabet as they learned the letters. Whenever a letter was mentioned, its sign was made. The amount of time devoted to signing and using the manual alphabet increased gradually at the same pace during each school year, documented by the teacher's lesson plans.

Testing Procedure

In this research as in the previous studies the PPVT-R was used to assess receptive English vocabulary. To measure the effect of the ASL treatment relative to the student's English vocabulary gains the PPVT-R, Form L, was administered as a pretest during the first week of school in September. At the end of the school year, during the third week of May, all those previously tested were retested, using the PPVT-R, Form M, to determine the extent of their vocabulary gain.

The PPVT-R was administered and scored in the conventional fashion. The standard score equivalent was calculated for each child. The age-referenced aspect of the PPVT-R takes into account normal vocabulary gain.

The pretest-posttest procedure was repeated in the same sequence with the classes during each of the two successive years. The students' receptive English vocabulary scores were compared to determine whether the teacher's greater experience with delivering instruction in ASL during the program's second year caused the students to achieve higher scores than the students had achieved during the program's first year.

A Sign Survey Questionnaire was developed to assess the impact of the ASL intervention in the out-of-school setting and to determine the children's and care givers' beliefs and behavior regarding sign language. After the posttest procedure was completed in school, the questionnaire was sent home with each of the thirty-four children in the program. The parents or primary care givers were asked to check the appropriate responses, add comments if they so desired, and return the completed questionnaire to the school with the child.

Results

In the first year the teacher used sign, the students earned the mean pretest score of 98.6 (sd, 13.21) on the PPVT-R, Form L, and the mean posttest score of 114.4 (sd, 13.09) on the PPVT-R, Form M. Results of a paired t test showed a significant difference between pretest and posttest scores (t, df 32 = -3.50; $p < .05$).

The second year the teacher used sign no significant difference was found between the morning and afternoon children's test scores on the Peabody. Therefore, data were collapsed into one figure representing a single mean for both morning and afternoon classes' pretest scores and a second figure representing a single mean for both morning and afternoon classes' posttest scores.

In the second year the teacher used sign the students earned the mean pretest score of 94.18 (sd, 13.55) on the PPVT-R, Form L, and the mean posttest score of 108.56 (sd, 14.48) on the PPVT-R, Form M. A paired t test showed a significant difference between the pretest and posttest scores (t, df 66 = -4.23; $p < .05$).

Year I and Year II pretest scores were compared. The mean pretest score for Year I was 98.6 (sd, 13.21) and the mean pretest score for Year II was 94.18 (sd, 13.55). A paired t test showed no significant difference between Year I and Year II (t, df 33 = 1.12; $p > .05$).

Year I and Year II posttest scores were compared. The mean for Year I was 114.4 (sd, 13.09), and the mean posttest score for Year II was 108.56 (sd, 14.48). A paired t test showed no significant difference between the Year I and Year II posttest scores (t, df 35 =

1.45; $p >.05$). The hypothesis was not supported by any significant increase in posttest scores from Year I to Year II.

The questionnaire was sent home with thirty-four children. It was completed by the primary care givers and returned to the school by twenty-six children. This 76 percent response rate is high and in itself meaningful. The Sign Survey's tabulated results indicate a favorable response to the sign language intervention in the out-of-school setting. Twenty people added comments on the survey. They are positive, comprehensive, and informative and are reported in their entirety. All the sign survey data from this study can be found in Chapter 5.

CONCLUDING THOUGHTS

Why was there no difference in student outcomes between Year I and Year II? The most logical and most probable explanation is that the addition of ASL to kindergarten curriculum of typical white students from the middle socioeconomic stratum can only provide a certain advantage. In each of my previous studies, the gain score students earned ranged from 13 to 16 points. The gain score represented in the present research is consistent with these figures. Year I (15.8) and Year II (14.8) fall within the expected range.

A teacher's additional ASL experience or presumed comfort with signing has been shown to have no effect on the size of the vocabulary gain score students will achieve. Although this finding does not support this study's hypothesis, it bodes well for the proponents of ASL instruction in early childhood education because, if this teacher's experience can be replicated by other teachers, the significant student vocabulary gains demonstrated could be achieved in the classroom with a minimal amount of teacher preparation. The cost of such teacher training should not be prohibitive, even given the current educational funding climate. The benefit to young learners would undoubtedly far outweigh the effort. Further support for this position would be my study "Seeing Language: The Effect Over Time of Sign Language on Vocabulary Development in Early Childhood Education" (discussed earlier in this chapter) which found that ASL-associated English vocabulary gains are sustained over a three-year period with no memory decay over time.

Examining the responses on the Sign Survey Questionnaire provides additional justification for ASL instruction. ASL has clearly precipitated participation by members of the child's household in the out-of-school setting and appears to be an effective communication component between home and school. It was indicated that all but one student enjoyed learning the signs and shared the signs with family and friends. The signs most often used by students were those that express actions and feelings. These categories of expression are critical to children's emotional development. Because of signs' iconic and kinesic properties, using sign language to express feelings culti-vates children's understanding of the fundamental nature of the feel-ings.

The written responses set forth a number of ancillary benefits the ASL instruction provided. It was noted that there were inherent social values displayed by the children. Learning a second language was viewed as an advantage, as was the realization that sign language is the language of people who cannot hear. The parents and care givers stressed the added excitement about learning they observed in the children and indicated a belief that learning sign language generated increased self-esteem; both of these parental views corroborate the observations expressed by teachers.

When you couple the students' significant vocabulary gains with the additional social and educational benefits delineated on the Sign Survey Questionnaire, it becomes apparent that there are multiple reasons to include ASL instruction in kindergarten curriculum. The endorsement of a relatively small number of parents becomes more weighty when their view clearly mirrors and echos the behavior teach-ers have observed and reported since sign has been a part of primary school education in Baltimore County and can become useful infor-mation for future curriculum decisions.

This study's specific finding that a kindergarten teacher's increased experience and presumed comfort with ASL instruction has no no-table bearing on student outcomes supports the notion that a minimal amount of preparation will provide a teacher with the medium needed to effectively incorporate this second language in kindergarten in-struction. ASL has been shown to increase typical hearing children's receptive English vocabulary, introduce a second language, enhance cultural awareness, generate self-esteem, and engender enthusiasm for learning.

In all of the research studies discussed in this chapter the use of ASL in classrooms with young hearing children has proved to give them an educational advantage. The information collected in these investigations should be especially beneficial for practitioners in early childhood education who are considering second-language learning or ways to enlarge the English vocabulary, communication skills, or verbal abilities of students. In addition, the narrative responses from the Sign Survey Questionnaire indicate parental beliefs and behavior may be meaningful components of this field of endeavor.

REFERENCES

Daniels, M. (1993). ASL as a factor in acquiring English. *Sign Language Studies, 78,* 23–29.

Daniels, M. (1994a). The effect of sign language on hearing children's language development. *Communication Education, 43,* 291–298.

Daniels, M. (1994b). Words more powerful than sound. *Sign Language Studies, 83,* 1–12.

Daniels, M. (1996a). Bilingual, bimodal education for hearing kindergarten students. *Sign Language Studies, 90,* 25–37.

Daniels, M. (1996b). Seeing language: The effect over time of sign language on vocabulary development in early childhood education. *Child Study Journal, 26* (3), 193–208.

Daniels, M. (1997). Teacher enrichment of prekindergarten curriculum with sign language. *Journal of Research in Childhood Education, 12* (1), 27–33.

Daniels, M. (in press). Sign education with young hearing children. *The Journal of Educational Research.*

_____ **Chapter 5** _____

Reactions of the Participants

How do the participants in the studies described feel about using sign language? Are the parents or primary care givers involved with sign outside school? Do teachers believe that including sign in hearing children's educational curriculum is worth the effort involved? And finally, what do the children think? This chapter offers the answers to all of these questions, often in the words of the parents, teachers, and students.

STUDENTS

There is a unique sixth-grade class in the elementary school in Windsor, Vermont, where sign language forms a portion of the students' instruction as a foreign language experience. The school district routinely elects to offer a foreign language component in its sixth-grade curriculum. Generally the language offered is Spanish, French, or German. Sign language is taught in this class because the teacher assigned to one of the sixth-grade sections knew sign language, and she was interested in teaching it and Deaf culture to her students for their foreign language experience.

Sign language is taught as any foreign language would be, but its nature lends itself to incorporating it in other aspects of the curriculum, such as songs and dramatic presentations, and in a more mundane manner sign also becomes very useful in classroom management. The students in this class were asked to write their thoughts about learning sign language. We seldom go to students for their input, and this is unfortunate, because they present a clear, perceptive view, from which educators can glean profound insights. The short paragraphs that follow are their own unedited work.

Callie: I really enjoy learning sign language, because when I am signing I feel like I'm learning a new perspective of looking at life and speaking with your hands. And sometimes when I feel sad or angry or sick, then I can sign it and I don't get embarrassed in front of the class. Last year when I saw the other kids sign I was in awe of how together and fluent they were and right then and there I knew I wanted to learn sign language.

Katelyn: The reason I wanted Mrs. Carmichael is because I could not wait to learn how to sign. Mrs. Carmichael is hard and is very ambitious. She keeps the days filled and when we go into sign language, I feel free and alive and that I can do anything. Sign to me is an art in its own way. I am going to miss doing sign language next year. I love sign language and I hope I can teach it when I get older.

Brandon: I think that sign language is a great language. It's easy to learn and use. And it is a lot easier than learning to pronounce different words. I think that it is neat that you can talk with your hands, and not always with your mouth.

Ashley: I think that everybody should have a chance to learn what sign language is and how to sign. If they don't learn sign language then they won't be able to communicate with other people who are Deaf.

   When I learn sign language I know that I am learning a different language. I love the way you can teach and learn sign language.

Lauren: Sign language is really neat, it's a whole new language I'm learning. Each time I do sign language with Mrs. Carmichael, I love it. It can get frustrating sometimes but it is worth it. Example: We did two class songs for a Variety Show in sign language and after we were done we got tears from people and standing ovations. It felt so good to see that other people care and love what we do. Sign language is an art, language, and a beautiful movement of the hands. I love it. Thank you Mrs. Carmichael. Sign language has let me communicate with the nonhearing and show others about it, it's wonderful!

Eric: I wanted to come to Mrs. Carmichael's class because she taught sign language. I feel happy when someone's teaching me sign. I go into a whole different planet when I am signing.

Bob: I wanted to have Mrs. Carmichael because she teaches sign. Learning sign is fun but difficult. I enjoyed learning sign.

Kyle: I think that sign language is a great thing. If more people start doing sign language then if a nonhearing person gets hurt you can understand what they're saying.

I think that every teacher should teach sign language so that most of the nonhearing people could come out and have something to do and people wouldn't stare, but instead they would try to communicate.

Kris: My comment about sign language is I like it a lot because I like learning other languages. My feelings about sign language are I like doing it and now I can talk to the people that can't hear.

Mariah: I feel very happy when I sign. Signing is special to me, because there are people out there that are deaf and are afraid to come out because they think hearing people won't understand them! I love to learn and do sign.

Greg: The reason I wanted to be in Mrs. Carmichael's class is because I wanted to learn Sign Language and so I can learn another language instead of just English. My feelings about signing are that you talk with your hands and not just your mouth.

Katrina: I think sign language is a fun way of talking with your hands. My feelings about sign are it makes me happy. It makes me happy because it is fun. My feelings about sign language are it makes me happy.

Micki Lee: Sign language is one of my favorite things I've learned. I wanted to be in Mrs. Carmichael's class because I have a cousin that was in her class and she liked it. Sign language is a good experience. I love using my hands as a language.

Other people want to learn it. I know this because I can see their hands twitching and their eyes widen. People have told me that it's the best when everyone is in sink [sync].

Sign language is a good way of talking without saying anything. When you're too sad to say anything you can express how you feel in sign language. Even if you just have a sore throat sign language is good. Sign language is like a whole 'nother world. Expression, movement, and detail.

These sixth-grade students have said a great deal about sign language. They understand that it is a language, and some recognize that sign may become an integral component in a future job. They see knowing sign as a way to provide comfort, acceptance, assistance, and additional communication avenues for people who are deaf. Their comments provide underlying evidence of positive mature attitudes toward diversity issues.

From their own perspective, they find sign helpful. It is easier for communication than difficult pronunciations; it is convenient when you have a sore throat; it is less embarrassing for delicate issues; it is great for expressing emotion. Conveying their deep inner feelings in sign seems to provide a certain magnum of solace. The prevalent sentiment expressed by the students concerned the happiness they feel when signing. The act of signing apparently takes them out of themselves so completely some believe they are on another planet. It seems a totally freeing experience.

My final comment regarding the reaction of these sixth-graders to sign language concerns the "fun but difficult" aspect, the "hard but worth it" comments. Knowing that you have to attend and work hard to achieve while realizing the rewards are worth the investment of your effort is a worthy outcome of this sign experience. What a powerful lesson to learn about gratification, within the context of children's elementary school education.

PARENTS

For nearly a decade sign language has been used in Maryland schools with typical hearing children; in early childhood education in prekindergarten and kindergarten, where it facilitates communication and classroom management and enhances vocabulary development; and in elementary school education in grades one through six, where it improves reading, vocabulary, and spelling and enriches the program in various other academic areas such as social studies and music. Throughout this time, teachers have consistently reported that sign language tends to precipitate participation in the children's education by members of the children's household and fosters interaction between the home and school.

To substantiate the teachers' perceptions a questionnaire was prepared for the student's primary care givers, designed to determine the reaction to the sign intervention out of school. This tactic garnered data to assess parental beliefs and behavior regarding sign language and discover whether the sign intervention did indeed have greater impact by engaging the family in the child's education. The questionnaire was also expected to ascertain whether sign language could reasonably be considered an effective communication avenue between home and school.

Two standard kindergarten classes were selected to receive the Sign Survey Questionnaire. Sign language constituted a regular part of the curriculum in these classes. (The classroom technique is described fully in Chapter 4.) In each class there were seventeen typical students of average ability and socioeconomic status, who all remained in their school program for the entire academic year. The Sign Survey Questionnaire was sent home with each of the thirty-four children before the summer vacation began. The parents or primary care givers were asked to check the appropriate responses; add comments, if they so desired; and return the completed questionnaire to the school with the child.

The questionnaire was completed by the primary care givers and returned to the school by twenty-six children. This 76 percent response rate is high, and in and of itself meaningful, showing an intense level of parental involvement. The Sign Survey's tabulated results, which follow, indicate a favorable response to the sign language intervention. Moreover, twenty people took the time to add written comments on the survey. These positive, comprehensive, and informative reactions are reported in their entirety.

Sign Survey/Tabulated Results

1. How has your child responded to learning signs?

   _25_ My child has enjoyed learning signs.
   _1_ My child has not expressed enjoyment or displeasure.
   ____ My child has not enjoyed learning signs.

2. Has learning signs been beneficial for your child?

   _25_ Yes, because
   _1_ No, because

3. Does your child share signs with you?

   <u> 25 </u> Yes
   <u>   1 </u> No

4. Does your child share signs with other children, neighbors, or family members?

   <u> 25 </u> Yes
   <u>   1 </u> No

5. Please check all categories that represent words that your child signs at home.

   <u> 17 </u> action words (talk, run, play, etc.)
   <u> 14 </u> animal words (cat, dog, horse, etc.)
   <u> 12 </u> color words (red, blue, yellow, etc.)
   <u> 14 </u> number words (one, two, three, etc.)
   <u> 16 </u> feeling words (happy, sad, excited, etc.)
   <u>   </u> poems
   <u>   8 </u> songs

Sign Survey/Additional Comments

1. My child learned how to communicate a different way.

2. It has made her aware of a whole other world. She now knows that not everyone hears, but they can still communicate. My daughter enjoyed showing me the signs she learned, but did not share them with me as much as my son did the year before.

3. My daughter tries to teach me sign language.

4. Sign language helped with language development and an awareness of different ways of communicating.

5. My son learned a very important lesson. He learned that there are children and adults that cannot hear and this is one way to communicate with them.

6. My daughter shows me how to use different words in sign language.

7. Tyler always comes home and shares what he has learned in sign language. The other day he showed me yes and no and asked if we could answer each other using the sign language he had just learned. Three cheers for teaching sign language. I sincerely hope it is continued.

8. I think this is a great program. It boosts my daughter's self-esteem by knowing something the rest of the family doesn't.

9. My son learned other ways of communicating, like going to the bathroom and be quiet.

10. Our daughter enjoys showing what she has learned to us.

11. Mark enjoys expressing himself with what he has learned from sign language.

12. My daughter will be able to speak to people who cannot and be able to understand them when they sign.

13. I think the extra experience is great. Kids find learning things like sign language easy and fun. It helps get children excited about learning, when it is something new and different.

14. Rebecca has learned a different way to communicate.

15. Diana remembers so much and she enjoys it a lot. The children are learning and don't even know it.

16. I think this is a beneficial communication tool. My child enjoys learning different things. When she says a letter she signs it.

17. She now knows there are other ways to communicate.

18. It is always beneficial for children to learn more ways to express themselves. Also, it is good for children to have two languages.

19. It teaches them that there are other ways to communicate besides talking. I would encourage this all through school, not just kindergarten. I think it is something that everyone should know, not just children.

20. I am extremely impressed with how well Lauren has done with signing. She truly enjoys it and is always excited to show off her talent anytime we are with someone new. I believe she knows she has learned something special.

When you read the responses on the Sign Survey Questionnaire you see that sign language has clearly precipitated participation by members of the child's household in the child's education in the out-of-school setting and does appear to be an effective communication component between home and school. It was indicated that all but one student enjoyed learning the signs and shared the signs with family and friends. The signs most often used by students were those that express actions and feelings. These categories of expression are critical to children's emotional development, and using sign language to express these feelings, because of signs' iconic and kinesic properties, cultivates children's understanding of the fundamental nature of the feeling. (More information concerning this subtle sign attribute can be found in Chapters 9 and 10.)

The written responses set forth a number of ancillary benefits the sign language instruction provided. It was noted that there were inherent social values displayed by the children. Learning a second language was viewed as an advantage, as was the realization that sign language is the language of people who cannot hear. The parents and care givers stressed the added excitement about learning they observed in the children and indicated their belief that learning sign language generated increased self-esteem; both of these parental views corroborate the observations expressed by teachers. The endorsement of a relatively small number of parents becomes more weighty when their view clearly mirrors and echoes the behavior teachers have observed and reported throughout the years sign has been an active part of primary school education in Maryland.

TEACHERS

The comments in this section are those of classroom teachers and reading specialists who teach reading with the use of sign language in Baltimore County, Maryland. Since the early 1990s, sign language has played an active role in the students' reading education. Because one hundred elementary schools in the county, each with its own reading specialist, are involved in a signing-for-reading-success initiative, the teachers' experience with signing is quite extensive and their insights, which follow, are important.

A reading specialist involved with students from kindergarten through sixth grade, when asked what she thinks about using sign language to teach reading to hearing children, responds:

It is a wonderful way. I can't teach beginning reading without using sign. Children have so much fun. It helps because they can see something they can associate with the sound. The sign actually seems to provoke their memory. So many of them have trouble remembering. In general, children's memories seem worse today than they were even a few years ago. We are seeing more students who are on medication for various conditions, often attention deficit disorder. Sign language is vital for them.

Another reading teacher used sign extensively during the six-week-long remedial summer school program. She offered these remarks:

I found sign was really helpful for those children, even for just the summer. The kids came in and they didn't really want to be there. The sessions were one and a half hours long, and the sign was a big inducement. It became a motivational thing for them. They could teach the signs to their parents and they enjoyed doing that. They, also, spontaneously cooperated and helped each other learn the signs. It was really a neat way to help the kids learn and retain their vocabulary and keep them involved over the hot summer.

A little seven-year-old boy with severe language impairment had just had a baby sister and he couldn't remember her name. He would come to school and I would say, "Jason what is the name of your baby sister?" Every morning he would come into school, and he couldn't remember the baby's name. It was *Courtney*. We kind of put together a little sign for her name to help him remember. (People who are deaf create similar sorts of name signs for each other so they do not have to resort to constantly fingerspelling acquaintances' names.) We would swing the tennis racquet for *court* which he could associate with his mom because she played tennis a lot, and slap his knee, for the *ny* part. For a while after that he would actually make the tennis swing and slap his knee, and then think and say *Courtney*. Before that he was not really able to retrieve the word. The cuing system was enough to make him remember the name. The kinesthetic motion seems to trigger a response and helps kids recall the word.

A third teacher responded:

I first used sign when I was a reading specialist and there were two or three little ones in first grade who weren't catching on to the word attack, the phonics, or anything. So I took them to my room and I started working with them on the manual alphabet, and then for sight vocabulary I would show them the sign and the written word and they seemed to catch on, and with a little repetition, they were able to sign and recall and after a while with enough signing of the basic vocabulary, they were able to transfer from the signing to the printed page, and it got them going. It allowed them to learn the vocabulary and gain confidence. I always spoke the word, signed the word, and showed the word. For the students it was doing the sign, hearing the word, and seeing the written word. So, it was the whole thing.

I have used it with first through fifth grades. It helped older children, as well. The children who couldn't learn the skills through the modalities presented in the classroom did pick it up with the signing. They were able to retain it because they had that extra modality. In the regular classroom where you have children of varying abilities, from average to below average, sign is a help as well. It does work and it does help. The children are involved. They really like it. Their whole body is involved. They have to watch and do.

A reading teacher, who was attempting to teach nonreading fourth and fifth graders, became interested in using sign language with her students because of her instructional assistant. The aide would join the reading teacher's class of learning-disabled students after she finished teaching a hearing-impaired signing class and she would still be signing. The students in the reading class were intrigued and would say, "Well how do you do that?" or "What are you doing? Tell me how to do that."

The reading teacher continues the story.

The students were picking up the sign and they were remembering it. So we started working on Dolch words (basic sight vocabulary) and we started at square one with these kids to teach them how to sign the Dolch words, and then how to put these words into sentences. And they were learning! And they were so enthused about it! So we then began to expand ourselves a little bit.

This was all trial and error type of thing. We sort of did this and then got it involved with some of the social studies and some of the science. And it was like I was looking up the words as much as the kids were, but it made it kind of like we were all learning at the same time. They were looking up the words because they were so interested in this and they were learning dictionary skills without even knowing it. We'd share and laugh and joke if we made a mistake. The kids do seem to remember better than the adults.

I found for me signing was a wonderful awakening, as I had struggled with languages in school. I took Latin in college because it was the lesser of evils; at least you didn't have to speak it. I found with signing I began to remember words and learn words. It was a wonderful experience. I find I am probably a visual kinesthetic learner; so this kind of fed into my own learning style.

Signing is a way to teach reading. I write the word or display the word, and I want them to say it and sign it, to combine it so they see it, hear it, and feel it. A true multisensory type of thing. I will have them sign to each other without voicing. I like them learning the sign for the receptive part of it as well as the expressive part, so they aren't only doing the signing, but reading the signing, also. Sign works to get and keep their attention. I like to have them use their motor skills. Signing gets their attention focused and their hands are busy and they seem so much calmer. It is great because they are all doing it together and enjoying it. It helps them learn and learning becomes fun.

More about teaching procedures related to reading is found in Chapters 3 and 10.

CONCLUSION

In this chapter you have read the reactions to using sign language in hearing children's education from parents, teachers, and students. They all apparently recognize the value in adding sign language to the educational process, and although each group notes specific advantages, some advantages seem to cut across age and engagement boundaries and appear on every group's list of benefits. Perhaps the most insightful group are the sixth graders, who, although young, were old enough to understand and articulate the sign experience from a child's point of view.

Their clear comprehension of the aid and comfort their own knowledge of sign language could provide for members of the Deaf community is quite significant for ones so young. You could imagine that children exposed in this manner would carry a lifelong sense and model of the rightness of inclusive behavior. The other attribute of sign that children found useful was its facility for expressing pure emotion, particularly in sensitive areas. Although the students undoubtedly realized they were receiving an academic benefit from the sign language, it was not the centerpiece of their comments and was rarely noted.

On the other hand, in their remarks the teachers stressed the students' improved academic performance. Of course, this would be expected. However, the teachers did mention that students acquired more self-confidence and more enthusiasm for learning, as well. The parents also noticed that self-esteem and interest in school had increased since the children were using sign language in their classes. The common area, the advantage that all three groups were cognizant of, was fun. They all mention that they find an inherent joy in signing. It is fun!

_____ Chapter 6 _____

Other Researchers' Studies with Typical Students

This chapter is devoted to exploring the research studies that other investigators have conducted concerning the beneficial effects sign language provides for typical hearing students. Typical students are everyday, garden-variety students. They have no special needs, they run the academic gamut from high to low, and they make up the major portion of the student body in any ordinary classroom.

There are not a lot of studies concerning sign language and these typical students. The first documented attempts to use sign language for educational advantage occurred in the early 1980s. During this era sign language was emerging from its dark period. Throughout the major portion of the twentieth century sign language was not considered to be a legitimate language and was out of favor even in many educational institutions for Deaf children.

Those in mainstream education became interested in sign language in the late 1960s, when William Stokoe and the linguists who followed him indicated that ASL is a true natural language with rules for generating grammatically sound phonological, morphological, and syntactical structures. Relying on this new stature, sign language returned to prominence and use in education for the Deaf, as well as acquiring a new role in general education as a foreign language for hearing students. A steadily increasing number of colleges teach and accept ASL. In 1987, California became the first state to permit high school students to use sign language to fulfill their foreign language requirements. During the following decade many other states followed California's lead. Today, ASL is the third most used language in the United States, after English and Spanish, and is widely used in academic settings. In fact a book and videotape, *Come Sign with Us*, by Jan C. Hafer and Robert M. Wilson (1990) were developed exclusively to assist elementary classroom teachers in providing their hearing students instruction in ASL.

Many of the first studies concerning sign use with typical hearing children centered on hearing children of Deaf parents. Characteristically, early studies of hearing children of Deaf parents would examine the order in which these children would acquire language. Was spoken English or ASL learned first? The other question researchers were interested in answering was whether the hearing children would acquire two distinct languages or would they just use the sign grammar to represent the English word.

One such study, reported by Ronnie Bring Wilbur and Michael L. Jones (1974), was a longitudinal investigation of three hearing children, with apparently normal linguistic development, who all had two Deaf parents. The children were M, 8 ½ months; D, 19 months, and K, 44 months old when the testing commenced. The videotaped data were collected for 2 ½ months. Parental written records of signs and baby-sitter records of spoken words before and during the video evaluation were included in the assessment for each child.

Results of the study reveal that before using speech or sign all of the children first fingerbabbled in the appropriate hand-near-shoulder signing position. Every child's signs appeared earlier than their spoken English. These signs passed through several stages of development. Initially they were usually formed in the right place, but with the wrong hand configuration and motion. Over time the children would gradually move to the correct hand configuration and motion.

When you review their vocabulary records at any given age, the new signs and the new words are different. The differences in the signs and spoken words at each age are interpreted as evidence that the children are learning both English and ASL as separate systems. When the oldest child's data are evaluated it is clear that she is not translating from one language to the other: She is maintaining and using two separate language systems.

Evidence provided in the study that supports this conclusion is the way she indicates that she sees herself on TV. There are certain sign phrases that cannot be translated by single words, just as there are English words that cannot be translated into single signs. K used one of these, a configuration in which the hand is held in a fist with the thumb and pinkie extended, held to the chest, then moved toward the TV set, then back to the chest; it was repeated several times to indicate, "I see myself on TV." She could have used any of several more English-like phrases, for which she knew the signs, such as "See myself on TV" or "That is me on TV," but she chose to express the idea in ASL.

The authors of this classic study of the language development of three hearing children with deaf parents concluded that when presented with both ASL and English, the children used ASL first. They reasoned that this possibly occurred because of the earlier maturation of motor skills. The ASL in no way delayed or interfered with the normal acquisition of English. The children appeared to be well on their way to a bilingual, bimodal use of two separate languages with all of the inherent cognitive benefits attributed to bilingualism.

Another interesting study of a hearing child's expressive communication when presented with language in two modalities is the story of Davey by Kathleen and David Holmes (1980). He was a hearing child of hearing parents, who were both professionals working in the field of deaf education. Children of interpreters and teachers are often exposed to sign language, hence become fluent in ASL, and are many times included in research projects. This just happened to be the case with one of the children in my first ASL study, who was a hearing daughter of a certified interpreter.

Davey's parents were both proficient in ASL, and they communicated with him from the time of his birth using both speech and sign. Initially this was accomplished by signing with one hand while holding him in the other arm. When crooning or babbling nonsense syllables to the baby they would fingerspell a sign equivalent; for example, "Oooh" was represented by a series of fingerspelled os. In addition to his parents, two deaf adults interacted with the infant, as well as numerous nonsigning hearing adults.

Davey's initial expressive communications were recorded by his mother or father. Utterances were noted as being signed, spoken, or spoken and signed. They were recorded from his first expressive communication, which occurred when he was twenty-six weeks, until he was seventeen months of age. The data were carefully analyzed and compared with data from a group of normally developing hearing children who received language input exclusively through an auditory modality.

Davey's first word was *Daddy*, which he signed at 6 ½ months of age. Perhaps because he had better gross than fine motor control, sign gained an early physiological advantage. As he acquired his first fifty words in the next 5 ½ months, his fine muscle control improved and he chose a combination of modalities.

Davey's first fifty signed and spoken communicative acts were imprecise. Among his first words were *ball, book, bunny, baby,* and *boat.* Each of these five *B* words was signed and spoken. The researchers conducting this study believe it would have been difficult to differentiate among all of his *B* words if the parents had only had the spoken output from Davey. If that had been the case, they would undoubtedly not have been able to provide appropriate feedback for his neophyte communicative attempts. By combining an imprecise sign with his imprecise speech his parents were able to distinguish among his communicative attempts and provide supportive reinforcement of his labeling efforts. They could offer specific positive feedback, such as "Yes, Davey that is a bunny," rather than repeated question responses like "What *buh* do you mean?"

When Davey's rate of language acquisition is compared with that of a contemporary group of normally hearing children who received language input only through spoken English, Davey is far ahead. He acquired his first 10 words more than three months earlier than the mean of the comparison group. He acquired his first 50 words nearly six months earlier than the comparison group mean. At seventeen months of age he knew 112 words, more than double the 50 words of the children who were Davey's peers. The results of this study show that access to a signed-spoken mode of communication apparently accounts for Davey's early acquisition of language and his larger than average vocabulary.

Two studies conducted by Philip M. Prinz and Elisabeth A. Prinz (1979, 1981) set out to examine the linguistic development, in ASL and spoken English, of Anya, a hearing daughter of a profoundly deaf mother and hearing father. Data were collected from the time Anya's first sign emerged, at age seven months, until the age of twenty-one months, when she was systematically and appropriately using both languages. Anya was videotaped at home interacting with her parents during thirty-minute monthly play sessions. Detailed notes were made during each observation and the videotapes transcribed by two experimenters within forty-eight hours. Additionally, between observations, all new words signed or spoken by the child spontaneously or in imitation of others were recorded in a diary.

Anya followed the pattern established by other hearing children who are simultaneously presented with signed and spoken language. She babbled with her hands before she babbled with her voice. She signed words before she spoke words. She developed an ability to code-switch easily and use the appropriate language with the appropriate parent.

Anya's first sign, *mama*, was made when she was seven months old. An examination of her lexical acquisition reveals that she consistently acquired and used more signs than spoken words as she communicated with others. Between the ages of seven and twenty-one months, she used 43 percent more signs than words. The authors offer a number of possible explanations for the emergence of signs before spoken words. It may relate to the earlier development and control of hand muscles than of vocal musculature and to the notion that signs are motorically simpler to produce. Also, the consistent visibility of signs in terms of their shape or orientation in space and movement has an appeal for children. Signs are 100 percent visible, compared with speech, which generally does not exceed 40 percent visibility on the lips.

The first phase of Anya's simultaneous development in English and ASL emphasized the child's early knowledge of word meanings. Her lexical acquisition in ASL and spoken English progressed through stages similar to those of hearing children learning two spoken languages. Initially Anya's spoken vocabulary complemented her sign vocabulary, with only a small overlap of words both signed and spoken. Furthermore, learning languages in two modalities did not interfere with her semantic development, but rather appeared to aid it.

At about nineteen months of age Anya was beginning to demonstrate a more conscious and deliberate ability to code-switch from one linguistic system to the other according to the communicative needs of the addressee. When communicating with her mother she would eliminate voicing, tap her mother's shoulder, or wave an arm in front of her face to gain attention and then proceed to use ASL. With her father and other hearing members of the family she consistently used spoken English and gradually signed less. The study describes Anya's ability simultaneously to learn two languages, and her subsequent facility in discriminating between these languages to select the one better suited to the communicator. This is quite a remarkable feat for a child who had been on this earth for less than two years and illustrates children's innate physiological propensity for learning language.

Another study in the same category that relates to the previous study about Anya is Denny L. Griffith's (1985) report concerning the language acquisition of a hearing son with deaf parents and an older deaf sister. The subject, Dave, is the only hearing member of the family; the investigation using videotape, observation, and parental interviews and records followed his language development from his seventeenth to his twenty-third month. Griffith compared Dave's vocabulary acquisition with Anya's, described in the Prinz and Prinz study. She found that language development was similar in the two children.

By twenty-one months of age Dave used twenty spoken words and twenty-seven signs. At the same age Anya used fourteen spoken words and twenty-four signs. Both children learned their first signs before their first words, acquiring vocabularies that exceeded those of typical children who are exposed to spoken English only. There was little redundancy of vocabulary in either child, indicating that ASL and English are acquired as two distinct languages.

From a rigorous analysis of Dave's communication, Griffith concludes Dave was able to communicate more complex information with ASL than with spoken English. Her finding supports Wilbur and Jones's earlier conviction that young children are cognitively capable of producing more complex language motorically in the gesture language of ASL than vocally in the voiced language of English. This judgment demonstrates a physiological bias for using sign language among young children.

Dave, in the same way as Anya, was able to mode-switch or mode-find, as Griffith names it. He used only sign with his father, who only signed with him, and sign and speech with his mother, who used both with him. Further evidence demonstrating this capability is the incident reported concerning the time when Dave, at twenty months of age, was left to play with a nonsigning student language clinician who was visiting his home. He displayed searching behavior with this stranger: first a sign, then a sign with a word, then a word. On the basis of the response he received he continued his interactions with the nonsigning student using only spoken words.

These examples of Dave's and Anya's communication techniques show how skillful these children were at applying the "person-language principle." Findings in each of the previous studies in this chapter suggest that hearing children of deaf parents when exposed to ASL and spoken English in their communicative environment readily learn two languages, easily and appropriately code-switch, and appear to have an increased rather than a diminished ability and desire to communicate with others.

The final study I describe in this section is a comprehensive research endeavor conducted by Michael Orlansky and John Bonvillian (1985), which tracked the language, cognitive, and motor developments of thirteen young children over an eighteen-month period. The subjects, normally developing hearing children, each had at least one Deaf parent, and the principal means of communication in their homes was ASL. The results of this thirteen-subject study mirrored the findings of the single-subject studies, but because it examined data from thirteen children, it had more weight as evidence because it used a larger sample and therefore generated a stronger response in the academic community.

The subjects' acquisition of sign language vocabulary was clearly accelerated when compared with established norms for spoken language development. The children used their first recognizable sign at an average age of 8 ½ months, had mastered a ten-sign vocabulary at a mean age of 13 months, and began to combine signs at 17 months. The comparable mean ages for spoken language development are 12 months for the first word, 15 months for ten-word vocabulary, and 21 months for combining of words. These results are consistent with previous findings of accelerated vocabulary and syntactic development in children learning a visuomotor system as a first language.

When considering the children's cognitive development, the results of this study suggest that the correlation between language skills and cognitive development may well be inaccurate. It has long been thought that completion of the sensorimotor period is prerequisite to language acquisition. The researchers found that these children were able to produce language and place names on objects well before they displayed the appropriate cognitive precursors for such language. They conclude that evaluations that focus on speech production, as a measure of linguistic development, may be underestimating the true linguistic ability of children.

The other area this study evaluated was the children's motor development. This portion of the research revealed a notably different trend than their previously documented accelerated vocabulary development revealed. In contrast, their attainment of motor milestones, such as sitting, crawling, standing, and walking, was within the expected age ranges of normal motoric development. Moreover, comparing an individual child's patterns of sign language growth and motor development showed that attainment of a new motor skill had no discernible effect on the child's rate of sign language acquisition.

These and other contemporary studies have provided researchers with the opportunity to evaluate and consider not only the value of bilingualism for hearing children, but the advantage of language learning in two modalities. Examining bilingual, bimodal language learning for typical hearing children took a different turn at the end of the twentieth century, when educators began experimenting with sign language as a means to accelerate or improve particular language arts abilities, such as spelling, vocabulary, and reading. Actually this idea was not new; in the middle of the nineteenth century David Bartlett (1853) taught Deaf children and their hearing siblings in a family school, in what might be considered an early model of inclusive education. He discovered that signing and fingerspelling not only helped the Deaf children learn English, but helped their hearing siblings as well.

One of the contemporary educators interested in experimenting with sign language as a means to achieve specific literacy advantages for typical hearing children was Robert M. Wilson, a Professor of Education and the Director of the Reading Center at the University of Maryland in College Park. He had been introduced to the idea of using sign with hearing children from Jan Hafer, one of his doctoral students. In a 1984 study she found that learning disabled hearing students learned sight words more easily when compared with the Fernald Method, a multisensory strategy which involved tracing words to be learned. In her single subject design with nine replications, Hafer concluded that signing was an effective teaching strategy because signs were iconic, thus emphasizing the meaning of the words to be learned; signs transformed learning into a multisensory experience, so important for young children; and signs were highly motivating, thus insuring attention and excitement in the students.

Dr. Wilson liked to interact with young students and conducted his own primary research. He tells the story that follows to explain his recognition of the potential of sign language (e-mail communication, October 27, 1997).

Oscar was in second grade and had no reading sight vocabulary. I decided to try a $N = 1$ study with him. I went to pick him up in his classroom and he was sitting away from the other children—"Too disruptive," the teacher said.

I started with my best language experience approach [LEA]—five lessons—at the end of each lesson I asked him to pick the ten words he would like to learn. He did and we practiced with those words and he left knowing them. When I picked him up the next day I started with a review of the ten words and he knew only one. By the end of the fifth lesson he was very disinterested. Then I started LEA with signing of the ten words he picked. When I picked him up the next day, he knew ALL TEN. The next day he knew nineteen of the twenty new words. The third day I went to pick him up and he was seated with the rest of the group. "What happened?" I asked. "Oh, he is behaving much better. When he comes back from working with you, he is so excited, I let him teach the signs to the class. Now they look up to him and have stopped teasing him." So much for my $N = 1$ study, but Oscar had made a breakthrough via signing.

A number of significant outcomes resulted from Dr. Wilson's fascination with sign language. He helped influence principals and teachers in Prince George's County, Maryland, to develop and carry out a project designed to answer the question, Does the addition of the sign for reading vocabulary assist students with a history of poor vocabulary retention in retaining the new vocabulary? Ten schools participated in this successful project and the results were published (Wilson & Hoyer, 1985).

In each of the schools, a first- or second-grade teacher identified one child who had a history of difficulty with vocabulary retention. The teachers generally implemented the program with several such students, but data were collected on only one child. The fourteen-week intervention followed this pattern. During the first four weeks of the study, teachers used the traditional basal approach to reading without any signing. In the next six weeks they taught using signing.

During this signing intervention period the teachers taught the children the sign for each new word as it was pronounced. The students practiced simultaneously signing and saying the words. The new words were reviewed in this way, each day, for the entire week. Then the teachers returned to traditional instruction for two weeks and completed the study with two weeks of sign instruction.

At the end of the fourteen weeks, the students were tested on the words taught with traditional instruction and on the words taught with signing instruction. The individual students' data from all of the ten schools were combined. The results from traditional instruction show that students retained 69 percent of their sight words. The results from signing instruction indicate that students retained 93 percent of their sight words. The educational significance of the students' sight word retention with the signing instruction was apparent to the teachers.

Dr. Wilson was impressed with these results; he not only published them in a concise book, *Signing for Reading Success* (1986), co-authored with Dr. Hafer, but enthusiastically shared them with other educators. One of these people was Dr. Cindy Bowen, who at the time was the director of reading specialists in Baltimore County, Maryland. She had been one of Dr. Wilson's advisees at the University of Maryland. He excitedly told her about the small study he had done with signing and reading instruction. She gathered together six to eight reading specialists for a meeting with Dr. Wilson. He explained his study to them. After listening to his tale, the reading teachers were interested in experimenting with sign and each tried it with their students, some with primary students, some with intermediate students. They all found that it worked.

Now, this group began to refer to itself as the Signing for Reading Success Study [SRSS] Group after the book by Hafer and Wilson of the same name. At the next monthly meeting of the reading specialists, the group described their experiences to the other reading specialists from the rest of the one hundred elementary schools in the county. During this meeting the reading specialists expressed a desire to proceed with a trial. Each school was given *The Comprehensive Signed English Dictionary*, and one hundred reading specialists embarked on an adventure with signing in 1990 (Cindy Bowen, e-mail communication, November 2, 1997).

The expanded SRSS group's endeavors from this point on are set forth in greater detail in an article, "The Signing for Reading Success Study Group: An Approach to Staff Development" (Bowen, Mattheiss, & Wilson, 1993). This account describes the plan the group adopted to meet the goals they established. Happily, four of their immediate goals were successfully accomplished within the first year.

The first of these goals was to develop and produce a signing video that showed teachers working with students using sign to read big books, distinguishing between fact and opinion, reciting the alphabet, reading key vocabulary words, and signing songs. The tape, *Signing for Reading Success*, which is no longer available, was created by Education Channel in Baltimore County Public Schools (BCPS). It would be the first of a series of three videos.

The group's second goal was to develop and produce a signing bibliography. This ultimately included research references, books, videotapes, and curriculum materials. It was distributed to each of the elementary schools in Baltimore County.

Primary research was their third goal. They conducted a survey to determine how many elementary school teachers in the system were using sign as part of their educational approach. The survey results indicated 192 teachers were using sign, and that more than 100 of them would be willing to demonstrate signing or talk with interested teachers.

Fourth, they wanted to develop a brochure. This materialized as a small booklet, "Signing: A Reading Intervention Strategy," which was created to carry essential information about signing. They met their final initial goal when the brochure was distributed to teachers, parent groups, administrators, and other interested parties in the county. Interestingly, all of these endeavors were accomplished without a special budget, through the efforts of this group of sincerely dedicated, highly motivated teachers and administrators.

During the following year one of the teachers involved in the project published an article describing her experiences with signing. In "The Silent Sounds of Learning: Using Signing to Reinforce Reading Skills," Maggie Sydnor (1994) encourages other teachers to try signing. She allays their fears by telling them they do not have to be fluent signers; they just need to be teachers who are willing to learn along with their students.

She enumerates the benefits she believes sign provides for emergent readers. Sydnor finds teaching children the sign for their sight vocabulary helps them distinguish between words that are graphically similar like *and* and *said, was* and *saw.* Signing minimizes confusion because the sign for each word is distinctive. In the same vein, signs often provide context clues because of their iconic nature.

In the typical classroom children commonly see, say, and hear words. Signing adds the dimension of movement to learning. It also raises the level of classroom assessment, as the teacher can see each child's response. If a child should hesitate it is obvious, and the teacher can provide immediate corrective feedback. The children also tend to copy each other, and positive modeling results.

She finds that signing is infectious as students quickly expand their ability from signing isolated words to signing phrases and sentences. They retain the words they encounter in their reading and are motivated to learn new words through sign. They realize they have a special language and delight in sharing it with their friends, siblings, and parents. In situations when a more able brother or sister can be taught to sign by a younger or less able sibling, signing can promote self-esteem. Sydnor remains keen on sign language's specific facility to improve hearing primary schoolchildren's reading skills and has witnessed ancillary educational and social benefits, such as heightened self-esteem, as well.

In the next research study I describe, we change geographic location and student age level. This article, "Sign Language and Hearing Preschoolers: An Ideal Match" (Reynolds, 1995), recounts the experiences of a university professor who normally teaches sign language courses to college students who are preparing to go into the field of Deaf education, as the professor endeavors to teach preschoolers. Her venture into teaching sign language to this younger age group began when her four-year-old daughter, Margaret, volunteered her to teach her classmates in nursery school. Margaret's mother had taught her to sign, and she wanted her new friends at school to learn the fascinating language she knew.

I include the material because this teacher's particular experiences qualify her to present a unique view of the relation of sign language acquisition and retention to student age level. She also clearly sets forth the type and extent of nursery school teacher preparation necessary to do the job well. This program is representative of many nursery and preschool programs throughout the country that include sign language instruction in their regular curriculum.

Over the two years Reynolds was actively involved in the project she found the young children's interest remained high, and the preschoolers had a much easier time learning sign than her older university students. This difference did not surprise her, because her adult students had sometimes taken their children to class; when this had occurred, the children would invariably end up assisting and correcting their parents as they practiced signs.

Preschoolers were able to retain the sign language effortlessly. She discovered this fact when the older children, after two years in preschool, moved into kindergarten, where they received no more sign language instruction. They missed the signing and wanted to be included in lessons again. When she resumed with them, after an eleven-month interval, she happily found they had not lost their sign language vocabulary or proficiency.

Reynolds believes it is not necessary for teachers to have a lot of training before they begin to include sign language in their curriculum with young children. Instructors who are learning sign language themselves can produce outstanding results. She stresses the novice should master the basic signs for each lesson before making the presentation, but she eschews perfection. Contact with other signers, often other teachers, can be helpful.

The final tale for this chapter is the experience of a kindergarten teacher, in East Los Angeles, who decided to incorporate sign language in her class as a way to teach her students how to read (R. Nishida, personal communication, May 13, 1998). Her students are mainly Hispanic; in most cases Spanish is their first language; they are from lower socioeconomic backgrounds and the entire class qualifies for the Title 1 free breakfast and lunch program. Historically they test low on any standard academic measure. They face almost unsurmountable odds, gangs are prevalent in the neighborhood, and violence is often witnessed by the children.

She was motivated to try this approach with her students because she was having little success with traditional methods and an incident that had occurred in a restaurant many years earlier had remained in her memory. Her own young children had become so happily occupied and engrossed with signing that she and her husband had been able to hold a quiet conversation. Also, she recalled that when she was a child she had loved communicating with her friends in secret codes; she believed signing was a kind of "secret" code that her students would enjoy.

When the children arrive in her class to start kindergarten, they enter school with almost nothing. She often wonders what these children have been doing for the past four or five years. Most cannot recognize their own name nor write it. They do not know the names or sounds for the letters of the alphabet. In fact, they often do not understand the concept of a word and are unfamiliar with print.

She found signing did interest her students; it was different, it was silent, and it forced her students to concentrate and attend. She has used sign language to teach reading for three years, and according to her, it really works! She uses an approach whereby the students see, hear, say, and sign the word, augmented with accompanying concrete objects or pictures to make the words more meaningful at the start of the process. As the students gradually acquire a signed vocabulary, sentences are formed from the words. The manual alphabet is taught, as the various letters of the alphabet are introduced with their corresponding letter name and letter sound. Phonics is incorporated as blends and digraphs are added. This helps the children begin to recognize new words by using elements that are already familiar to them.

Her students do remarkably well. The last class I have records for were measured with the Gray Reading Test in April 1998. This was a huge class of thirty-one students, made up of twelve girls and nineteen boys. At the time of their testing, a normal grade level reading score would be 0.7. In her class of thirty-one students, twenty-eight children were reading English at grade level or above. Four children were reading at a 2.0–2.2 or second grade level. An amazing nineteen children were reading 1.1–1.9 or first grade level. Five children were right on grade level, 0.7–0.9 or kindergarten level, and only three children were below grade level. Anyone even remotely aware of the conditions in this school district would be utterly awed by the results of this reading assessment. I want to point out clearly that twenty-three of these students were able to read at a first-grade level while they were still in kindergarten.

The teacher in East LA was experiencing the same positive results of using sign language with her students that Dr. Wilson had encountered with Oscar nearly twenty years before. This kindergarten teacher knows sign helps children recognize letter shapes and sounds, remember word names and meaning, and, ultimately, learn how to read. Dr. Wilson also knows signing enhances hearing children's literacy. All of the other teachers described in this chapter can attest to the academic benefit sign language silently provides. This benefit moves beyond simply enriching hearing children's education. When the magnitude of the sign advantage is carefully considered, and one looks at the meaning of test results in context, it is clear that use of ASL is a strategy that offers untold promise for students who can ill afford to be denied any longer.

REFERENCES

Bartlett, D. (1853). Family education for young deaf-mute children. *American Annals of the Deaf and Dumb, 5*, 32–35.

Bowen, C., Mattheiss, J. H., & Wilson, R. M. (1993). The signing for reading success study group: An approach to staff development. *Literacy: Issues and Practices, 10*, 48–52.

Griffith, P. L. (1985). Mode-switching and mode-finding in a hearing child of deaf parents. *Sign Language Studies, 48*, 195–222.

Hafer, J. (1984). *The effects of signing as a multisensory technique for teaching sight vocabulary to learning disabled hearing students.* Unpublished doctoral dissertation, University of Maryland.

Hafer, J. C., & Wilson, R. M. (1986). *Signing for reading success.* Washington, DC: Gallaudet University Press.

Hafer, J. C., & Wilson, R. M. (1990). *Come sign with us.* Washington, DC: Gallaudet University Press.

Holmes, K. M., & Holmes, D. W. (1980). Signed and spoken language development in a hearing child of hearing parents. *Sign Language Studies, 28*, 239–254.

Orlansky, M. D., & Bonvillian, J. D. (1985). Sign language acquisition: Language development in children of deaf parents and implications for other populations. *Merrill-Palmer Quarterly, 31* (2), 127–143.

Prinz, P. M., & Prinz, E. A. (1979). Simultaneous acquisition of ASL and spoken English in a hearing child of a deaf mother and hearing father: Phase I, early lexical development. *Sign Language Studies, 25*, 283–296.

Prinz, P. M., & Prinz, E. A. (1981). Acquisition of ASL and spoken English by a hearing child of a deaf mother and a hearing father: Phase II, early combinational patterns. *Sign Language Studies, 30*, 78–88.

Reynolds, K. E. (1995). Sign language and hearing preschoolers: An ideal match. *Childhood Education*, Fall, 2–6.

Sydnor, M. H. (1994). The silent signs of learning: Using signing to reinforce reading skills. *Literacy Issues and Practices, 11*, 30–37.

Wilbur, R., & Jones, M. (1974). Some aspects of the acquisition of American Sign Language and English by three hearing children of deaf parents. In La Galy, Fox, & Bruck (Eds.), *Papers from the Tenth Regional Meeting of the Chicago Linguistic Society*, 742–749.

Wilson, R. M., & Hoyer, J. P. (1985). The use of signing as a reinforcement of sight vocabulary in the primary grades. *1985 Yearbook of the State of Maryland IRA, 1*, 43–51.

Chapter 7

Children with Special Needs

In this chapter I focus on some of the newer programs in which sign language is being implemented for children with special needs. Young normally developing children happen to be the main focus of this book; however, children with special needs are included because sign's proliferation among these students is assuming some fresh and interesting forms that may be helpful for typical children as well. Historically, sign language has proved useful for language-delayed, language-disordered, and learning-disabled populations. Typically, specific signs have served as gestural cues for children with communicative impairments, for children with Down syndrome, for children with aphasia, and for children with autism. Using sign language as a communicative tool with educationally challenged hearing children improves their communicative competence and academic ability.

I was first aware of this in the mid-1970s, when my daughter served as a counselor at a camp for special needs children. All of the staff received sign language instruction as part of their training and routinely used sign language to communicate with many of the campers. Sign was the signal for *stop, line up, sit, bathroom, hungry, tired, sick, thirsty*: all of the many management words and phrases. Because sign was the way the nonverbal children normally communicated, and there were many of them, it was quickly picked up and adopted by the rest of the campers and soon became the usual way for everyone to communicate, unofficially becoming the official Camp Rainbow code or language.

In the years since my daughter's camp experience, there has been a greater acceptance of ASL as a language in the general population and a more extensive use of sign with special needs children. A program initiated in the early 1990s at the Clinical Genetics and Child Development Center of Dartmouth Hitchcock Medical Center in Hanover, New Hampshire, uses sign language with children who have Down syndrome to enhance their verbal skills.

The center's research findings were highlighted in their program report presented at the International Early Childhood Conference on Children with Special Needs (Gibbs, Springer, Cooley, Aloisio, 1991). The researchers found that engaging the children's families in signing programs and encouraging them to use sign language consistently when they communicated with their children, helped the children to make significant progress in their use of verbal expressive language. Without the use of sign the children's true expressive language ability would not have been apparent. Sign helped the parents recognize their child's word approximations and served to expand their overall vocabulary.

The children began the program when they were twelve months of age. Extensive records of both their use of signs and verbal words and their parents' use and knowledge of signs were maintained throughout the treatment. The children's total vocabulary, both verbal words and signs, was evaluated when they were twenty-four months of age and compared with the number of signs their parents knew and used with them. The results show a high correlation between the parents' and children's use of signs.

Each family was encouraged to expand their use of sign to the level they felt comfortable with by using meaningful functional signs that could easily be incorporated within their daily routine such as *more, all done, eat,* and *drink.* The parents' practice of consistent sign use appears to have a positive effect on their child's expressive language acquisition in both modalities. The child's ability to respond to sign seems to reinforce and stimulate the parent's use of sign in an escalating fashion.

Most families reported that sign increased their child's capacity to attend. They also believed sign aided comprehension and served to facilitate communication exchanges between parent and child. The parents felt their child's needs and desires were easier to understand and there were fewer frustrating dialogues.

There was a wide range, between a low of nine and a high of seventy, in the number of words each child knew by the time they were two years old. However, on average each of the eleven children in the study acquired a twenty-five word vocabulary by age two years. Surprisingly, the size and range of their vocabularies compare favorably with those of typical children. In addition, all of the evidence collected clearly indicates that sign does not hinder the emergence of verbal ability. The results of programs like this have generated a greater reliance and a stronger confidence in the use of sign language for children with Down syndrome.

Laura Feltzer, a teacher at Perez Special Education Center in East Los Angeles, uses sign language to teach her class of eight- and nine-year-old trainable mentally retarded (TMR) students to read. Usually such students are not considered likely candidates for reading instruction, and their reading education is usually limited to what would be considered survival reading. However, these children are learning to read for pleasure by correlating signs with written words and phonics.

According to an article in the *Los Angeles Times* (Marroquin, 1999), Feltzer started introducing sign language to reading classes ten years ago, after she found her hearing students signing along with some deaf classmates in her class at that time. She later experimented and discovered that using sign was a successful strategy for teaching her TMR students to read. Feltzer says, "Certain motions trigger certain words." The main feature of her program is that students learn to read by not only seeing, hearing, and saying printed words, but by signing them.

I spent a day observing Feltzer in her classroom in April 1999 and was impressed with her students' reading abilities. They are interested and involved in the process. They normally stay in her classroom for two academic years, so some of the children had been with her a full year longer than their classmates. The children who had been part of her class for nearly two years were able to read popular books such as *Hop on Pop* and *Green Eggs and Ham* easily, without any help.

Several of these students were asked to read their current favorite book aloud to their classmates. During their reading, Feltzer would stop the reader and check the children listening for comprehension. Their responses showed the entire cohort stayed remarkably focused

on the reader and the content of the book. The entire class was involved and stayed on task. I am well aware that I was an audience,
and in essence, they were strutting their stuff, but even taking that
into account, it was a very imposing demonstration.

Feltzer continued her demonstration by showing me how she
teaches her students their new vocabulary words. There were nine
children sitting in a semicircle and each learned a word. At this juncture, in their ongoing instruction, she selects the individual words she
wants to teach them from books they are reading or from books she
has created for them to read.

On the day I was there, I saw her teach *my, eat, run, under, flower,
grandmother, nice, picture*, and *toy*. When she is teaching a word, she
says the word, shows the child a card with the written word, displays
an action or object that represents the word, and teaches the child
the ASL sign for the word. She went around the circle, and each
child learned to sign and say their new word when she displayed the
word card. The word cards were reviewed at the conclusion of the
circle learning period, and again at the end of the day. By this time,
all of the children were able to read their written word without hes-
itation and make the appropriate sign for the word.

This process is repeated day after day as the children review their
words from the previous day and learn their new word. Each child
proceeds at their own individual rate, and Feltzer is careful not to
introduce additional new words until she believes the student can
successfully read their current sight words with ease. Using sign as a
tool, these children become readers.

Feltzer's reading program engenders confidence and a sense of accomplishment in her TMR students, who typically have either Down
syndrome or autism. In this classroom, sign language moves beyond
its initial use as merely a communication device for children with
special needs to fulfilling an academic role in reading instruction and
offering these children an opportunity to feel good about themselves.

In another part of the country, sign language continues to be used
to help children learn how to speak. The *Richmond Times-Dispatch*
(Lohmann, 1999) reports that teachers in a special needs prekindergarten program at Nuckols Farm Elementary in western Henrico
County, Virginia, are finding sign language a most effective tool for
their students. They are having great success with children who have
experienced language delays. These children, often diagnosed as
having autism, have no discernible hearing problems but are slow to

talk. The teachers use sign language to communicate with them. They use signs as visual cues, as a means of making it easier for children to follow directions, as a way to help children make connections between words and concepts, and ultimately as a method for leading them to speak.

One such student, featured in the article, is Chase Scott, who was a 3 ½-year-old nonverbal child when he entered the program. He actually spoke his first word in school. One afternoon as he caught sight of his mother when she arrived to pick him up from school he unexpectedly blurted out, "Mommy!" Of course his mother as well as all the others who were there witnessing the emotional scene cried. According to his mother, in less than a year, Chase is now starting to say sentences and has a vocabulary of hundreds of words. His teacher, Terry Powell, says: "I truly believe it is through sign language that his (verbal) language emerged."

All of the teachers in this prekindergarten program routinely use sign language to communicate with the students. The vast majority of the student population has been diagnosed with autism. Children who have autism have great difficulty processing verbal information and do far better responding to visual communication. Sign language, pictures, or pictographs illustrating the steps of a task are much easier for them to understand than words. Language appears to be jumbled in their heads, and sign language gives them another piece in what for them is a very confusing puzzle. And as in the case of Chase it often helps them develop their verbal language as well.

This article is comprehensive in nature and indicates several other programs in the greater Richmond area where sign language is meeting various educational demands for populations who have special needs. It is being used as an aid to teach spelling at the Virginia Treatment Center for Children, where the principal, Dr. Shirley Wiley, describes sign as a trigger to retrieve stored information in students' brains. She finds sign language requires students to remain attentive to the teacher and helps keep them on task. She requires her staff to learn sign language in order to teach the children in the center more effectively.

Sign is also proving helpful, according to Lisa Wright, a speech pathologist at Virginia Commonwealth University, for the language-delayed children with whom she works. She finds sign language reduces frustration, eliminates negative behavior and functions as a communication bridge.

The *Boston Globe* (Wong, 1999) featured an article about a residential special needs school and treatment center in Needham, Massachusetts, where sign language is used to help students focus, calm down, and communicate. The Walker Home and School has adopted a new and innovative program in which all of its eighty students are taught ASL. The children, ranging in age from five to thirteen, are a challenging student body with a variety of difficulties, ranging from abuse and neglect to learning disabilities and developmental disorders, who were unable to succeed in other programs. Often, they have suffered through a series of foster homes and some have been in psychiatric hospitals.

The program is largely the brainchild of Ira Kittrell, a speech pathologist, who was added to the staff to get violence in the school under control. Kittrell learned sign language many years ago and used it to teach students with special needs in a junior high school in New York, where he noticed it helped his students pay closer attention to him. Later, he implemented sign with children and stroke patients in his one-on-one speech therapy sessions.

When he began to work at Walker in 1998 he was aware sign language could be useful with students who have special needs, but the program that he developed and now runs came about as a result of happenstance. This seems to have been the case with many of the programs I have written about in this book. Often the element of chance or luck plays a role, but the consistent impetus in the various applications is always the signing.

In Kittrell's situation, a female student saw him signing to another teacher. She asked him to teach her how to sign. He agreed and began teaching her in the school lunchroom; soon other students asked to join, and before long fifteen students were attending the lessons. The instruction proliferated in a more regular format, and now all younger students receive a half hour of special sign instruction every week, and the older students learn the language in their weekly social skills classes.

Several examples of what occurs in real situations are recounted in the article. In one instance, an emotionally disturbed child suffering from an anxiety attack uses sign language to remind himself to be careful and asks for permission to be close to someone else. Given the same circumstance, before the sign program, this child would have impulsively thrown himself into another person without realizing he was encroaching on personal space. This sort of action often would have led to a disagreement or fight, which could very readily escalate into a major confrontation.

In another example, a child is removed from a classroom after an emotional outburst. He is in the hall, so upset he is unable to say what is bothering him. When approached by Kittrell the boy is able to express his difficulties in sign language, and the predicament is resolved. Before the introduction of sign language, in an instance such as this, the child would frequently become violent and spiral out of control, sometimes to the point of requiring physical restraint.

Richard Small, Walker's executive director, says the number of times staff had to restrain children who were acting out or violent physically dropped 27 percent from 1998 to 1999. He credits their new sign language program for the reduction in violence. As quoted in Wang, Small says

I agree with all the people who say anytime you do a restraint it is potentially very dangerous, and we would like to eliminate it. It is no accident that the kids who get involved in this extreme violence, like out in Colorado, are so isolated and detached that they are totally out of connection with their peers and adults.

Parents and staff report that since the implementation of the sign language program students are better able to communicate with each other and the staff, and they can usually identify their emotions and act on them appropriately. Students say they think signing is fun and they find it to be an easier way to communicate; some indicate they are visual people and say when they see something they can remember it more easily than when they hear or read it. Signing has caught on to such a degree at Walker that one school assembly was conducted with sign language and followed by signed applause.

This program is quite unique; in fact Dr. Raymond Yerkes, co-chairman of the American Academy of Child and Adolescent Psychiatry's residential treatment committee, says he is unaware of a similar program elsewhere in the United States. However, the benefit sign gives these children with special needs has also been observed by teachers working with typical children. Many such teachers have found that when they incorporate sign language in their instruction, there is less conflict in the classroom, their students more readily express their feelings, and they tend to communicate more freely.

I close this chapter with yet another population having special needs who are receiving an educational advantage from sign language. In a public school in Pontiac, Michigan, a third-grade class of predominately Hmong children are learning ASL in order to learn English. This is not occurring as the result of a special new program; it is happening because their teacher, Carol Analco, who is a fluent signer, thought it might work. As the mother of eight-year-old deaf twins, she is a seasoned signer and well aware of the way her twins are learning English through their native ASL.

Analco's Hmong students are all limited English proficient (LEP). These students were born in Laos, Thailand, or Vietnam and were refugees of the Vietnam War. The Hmong helped the Americans during the war by translating and by guiding them through the terrain they knew. Because they lost their country, Laos, and did not want to live under a Communist regime, they immigrated to the United States. The last refugee camp in Thailand closed in about 1997, and the Hmong were all moved together to Pontiac or to other places in the United States where they had relatives. Additional large concentrations of Hmong can be found in Fresno, Minneapolis, and Milwaukee.

Analco believes her third-grade students could easily pass an ASL 101 class. She teaches them sign and uses a lot of sign with them and finds it helps them learn English. There are many English words her students do not know, and for many of these words there is no comparable word in Hmong. She uses ASL, and Analco's theory is that with the ASL picture in their minds, her students are able to make the connection between the sign and the English word.

Analco discovered just how much her Hmong students' English vocabulary had increased when they were given the Language Assessment Survey (LAS), which is given to limited English proficient (LEP) students twice a year, in early fall and at the end of the school year, to access their oral and written comprehension of the English language. In the fall, her students were at the lowest standing. All students scored a level A, which indicates that their skills in English were not fluent, and they could not comprehend English.

When Analco received her students' scores from the June testing, she was gratified to discover, that they had all jumped two to three levels. Everyone went from the lowest level of an A to a C, D, or E on the LAS. The person who did the testing, shocked, asked Analco, "What have you been doing?" When the principal learned about Analco's students' scores, she was really surprised and told her to keep doing whatever she was doing.

Analco's students' English language achievements are even more remarkable when they are compared with the results from the school's other third-grade class. The other class consisted mainly of higher-functioning third-grade Hmong students who had C or D scores on the LAS in the fall. In addition to their higher initial scores, this class received the benefit of one hour a day of special English as a second language (ESL) instruction. However, when this third-grade class was tested in June they earned really poor scores: some stayed at the same level, the level of one went down, and the level of the rest increased only one level (C. Analco, e-mail communication, June 18, 1999).

This teacher's successful ASL intervention with her Hmong third graders was the result of happenstance. We have often seen this to be the case in other programs in this chapter, which has covered a wide range of children with special needs. Sign language, in its varied applications, has proved useful in a variety of settings. Sign is effective in New Hampshire with children with Down syndrome, where it is serving as a means for them to learn their first vocabulary words. Sign is helping TMR students in California learn how to read. Sign is an avenue to articulation for nonverbal children in Virginia. Sign is preventing violence and aiding both intrapersonal and interpersonal communication in a residential home for troubled children in Massachusetts. And sign is a valuable tool for Hmong students learning English in Michigan.

REFERENCES

Gibbs, E. D., Springer, A. S., Cooley, W. C. & Aloisio, S. (1991, November). *Early use of total communication: Patterns across eleven children with Down Syndrome.* Paper presented at the meeting of the International Early Childhood Conference on Children with Special Needs, St. Louis, MO.

Lohmann, B. (1999, April 7). A time to speak. *Richmond Times-Dispatch,* p. D1.

Marroquin, A. (1999, February 21). Motions that motivate. *Los Angeles Times,* p. B2.

Wong, D. S. (1999, May 1). Sign language helps troubled youths. *Boston Globe,* p. B1.

Chapter 8

Inclusive Programs

This chapter focuses on programs that integrate typical children who hear with children who are deaf in the same classroom. This mainstream or inclusive education represents the future for many children who are deaf. There remains controversy in the Deaf community regarding this shift in educational policy, instigated in large part by the passage of the Americans with Disabilities Act (ADA) and the legislation that followed.

There are those who believe that inclusive education is not the least restrictive education for children who are deaf, as the ADA promises. These people feel, and I tend to agree with them, that placing children in an environment where they will not encounter others using ASL, which is their native language, is an extremely restrictive environment. Spanish-speaking children placed in English-speaking classrooms still have the opportunity to process information and think in their native Spanish at home with their Spanish-speaking families. For children who are deaf this opportunity does not exist, as in 90 percent of the cases, children who are deaf are members of hearing families with whom they are unable to communicate. The native language of such children is often not established in the home, and they have no code or language to use for inner speech or intra-personal communication, so important, actually downright necessary, for thinking and development.

A child who is deaf needs to interact and establish a native language from other ASL users. This process has traditionally been the function of residential schools. If the present trend continues, and more and more children who are deaf receive their education in inclusive mainstream settings, it will become increasingly important for a larger number of their hearing classmates to know how to communicate with them in ASL or some form of sign language.

I will explore three representative inclusive programs. The first, in an elementary school in Alaska, dates from the early nineties. The second, in a primary school in the United Kingdom, covers a mid-nineties pilot program, for which I served as a consultant and am therefore able to offer a fairly detailed account. The third, in a university-related preschool in Louisiana, was published in the late nineties and clearly depicts what occurs in a large number of integrated early childhood educational initiatives in the United States today.

The program in Fairbanks, Alaska, was called Multigraded Education for Deaf and Hearing Students (MEFDAHS). "Mef-duz," as it affectionately came to be known, was the brainchild of Lynn Gilbert, who conducted extensive research and presented a proposal to the school board. In 1991, Gilbert received approval and funding for a three-year inclusive multigrade program.

The program was designed for students in grades one through six. They were divided into two classes: grades one through three and grades four through six. Of course, the numbers of individual students in individual classes varied from year to year, but in general there were twenty-five children in each of the two classes. The usual makeup in each class would be ten children who were deaf and fifteen children who were hearing.

The MEFDAHS teachers were all hearing, although there was a strong effort to include native signing adults who were deaf in the program. These adults served as resources for the teachers. In addition, volunteers from the local Deaf community participated with instruction in the classroom on a regular basis. As the program progressed, there was an ongoing active exchange of ideas among the teachers and volunteers. Once a month, the program teachers and the Deaf community members sat down with each other to share experiences, opinions, and lunch.

The principal teaching tool was a twenty-minute-long videotape, which was viewed in class each Monday and then sent home with the children. The tape consisted of the new vocabulary, spelling, and reading words for the thematic unit presented in both sign and voice and by a word written on a card held by the person in the video. When the tapes arrived at home, the parents learned the signs and practiced with the students. This procedure also kept the parents abreast of the unit topics being covered.

At the end of the video there was a weekly "Catch a student being good" vignette. This was a short summary, entirely signed in ASL with no voicing, about a student who had been observed showing wonderful megaskills. Megaskills were eight lifelong skills that the curriculum focused on throughout the year: responsibility, initiative, caring, creativity, perseverance, independence, cooperation, and problem solving. The children and the parents were eager to watch the video each week to see whether they had been chosen to be the highlighted student who had been caught displaying a megaskill.

For the children who were hearing, the program was an immersion into the language. ASL became the primary language in the classroom. By Thanksgiving, all of the children were proceeding nicely with their ASL. By Christmas, they were all fluent signers. They were learning the language by understanding the concepts and actually using ASL daily, rather than learning from just a list of ASL vocabulary.

The students who were Deaf had the tapes as well. They wanted to be equal in skills to the children who were hearing, so they worked hard. For the Deaf students, the tapes provided an opportunity to practice reading and speech reading. All the students were treated in the same way, and the tapes appeared to provide a parallel benefit for both hearing and nonhearing participants. The three-year-long program had high expectations, which were met squarely, to the delight and amazement of all.

This innovative Alaskan program was a wonderful success. The hearing children all achieved and made remarkable advances, learning not only specific curriculum, but ASL as well. In fact one child is going on to become an interpreter and several others are leading sign clubs. All have retained their ASL skills and their affection for and affiliation with the Deaf community. The Deaf children also learned the unit contents, but, most importantly, they learned English and gained hearing signing friends who can communicate with them in ASL. Multigraded Education for Deaf and Hearing Students remains an outstanding example of an inclusive educational endeavor that works (G. Litzen, e-mail communication, February 4, 1998).

Sign in Education was a pilot program conducted in the United Kingdom that integrated Deaf children and hearing children in a hearing classroom with a culturally Deaf teacher who taught the national curriculum to the pupils, both Deaf and hearing, in British Sign Language (BSL) for one afternoon a week throughout the fourteen-month-long project.

BSL is analogous to ASL in the United States. It is the native language of British people who are deaf. Remember, there is no universal sign language that would be understood worldwide, and any country with a sizable Deaf population is likely to have its own sign language (see Chapter 2).

The British program paired students from two schools in the same community. They were St. Thomas More RC Primary School, Middlesbrough, and Beverley School for Deaf Children, Middlesbrough. Every Monday afternoon six Deaf children from Beverley School, their teacher, and their classroom assistant were transported to St. Thomas More, where they joined a year 1 class (first grade) of nineteen hearing students and their classroom teacher.

A BSL tutor employed by the project would be in the classroom during these afternoons and became the focal point of instruction as she conducted the majority of the lessons for all of the children in BSL. In addition, the BSL tutor spent two more days each week working alongside the hearing teacher with the hearing students in the classroom at St. Thomas More.

The tutor's first language is BSL, written English her second. She uses no spoken English, was born deaf, and is a descendant of five generations of Deaf people. The BSL tutor sees and experiences the world from a Deaf perspective. The teacher's having these insights was deemed important for the integrated situation, and she was selected for the position because she was a culturally Deaf native signer.

The project was developed by Kathy Robinson, a hearing primary school teacher who is the mother of two daughters who are deaf. She believes that the responsibility to communicate in the primary school classroom should be borne more equitably by hearing and deaf children. At present 90 percent of all deaf children in the United Kingdom are integrated into mainstream schools, where they are expected to communicate in English. The burden is placed solely on deaf children, who cannot use their own language (BSL) and must instead learn to use English. Robinson feels that hearing children should acquire the wherewithal to communicate with deaf children in their natural language, BSL.

She was able to convince others of the merit of her view, and the research initiative Sign in Education, designed to develop BSL skills in hearing children, gained financial support from the Royal National Institute for Deaf People, Teesside Training and Enterprise Council, and a number of businesses. The research program, which was the first of its kind in the United Kingdom, monitored and assessed the hearing children's acquisition of sign language, the relationships between deaf and hearing children, and the attitudes of the staff and children.

Sign in Education had five specific aims: It was designed to support teaching of the national curriculum to Deaf and hearing pupils with BSL; to develop BSL skills in hearing children; to integrate Deaf children into mainstream classrooms; to develop Deaf awareness and a positive attitude toward Deaf people; and to develop appropriate resource materials to enable Deaf children and children without hearing impairments to experience a visual-spatial language (Robinson, 1997, p. 1).

One of the program's greatest strengths was its ability to cope in a freewheeling manner with events as they occurred in uncharted waters. Interviews with all personnel before the start of the program suggest they were unsure about what would happen but were willing to work together on the project. The concluding interviews indicate that they all found the program worthwhile, and have some specific insights and suggestions.

The following material provides a thumbnail sketch of each of the three educators directly involved in curriculum delivery with the children in the project. Included are a bit of individual background and an attempt to discern their pre- and postprogram beliefs. Their precise suggestions are highlighted by relaying them in their own words. These comments give a clearer picture of what transpired during the Sign in Education Project.

The teacher of the Deaf traveled with six of her students from the deaf school to the hearing school, where they were integrated in the hearing classroom. Her aims for her students were the expected inclusion, social confidence, improved communication, speech, and understanding. When she reviews the project and the progress her charges have made, her focus changes somewhat and she focuses a good deal of attention on BSL. In the integrated setting her Deaf students have had much greater exposure to BSL than they had previously. The BSL tutor uses it exclusively, and as the program progressed, the tutor did more and more of the teaching. When the teacher of the Deaf teaches at the Beverley School for Deaf Children, she uses Sign Supported English (SSE) with her class, not BSL. She notes that teaching by a person whose first language is BSL provides a unique support that a hearing teacher of the deaf cannot supply: "It gives the children the opportunity to see and learn Sign" (Robinson, 1997, p. 18).

She observed that BSL benefited both the hearing and the Deaf children. She noticed that BSL helped the hearing children develop their reading skills. This, she noted, was particularly true of the less able hearing readers, whose reading she felt became more confident with BSL. She reasoned that BSL gave the hearing students something concrete to pin the words on. She said it was possible to see this reading development.

Her fondest memory of social development and communication was the sight of four (Deaf and hearing) children huddled together around a table discussing what they liked about a comic book one of the children had been given for Christmas. The BSL conversation was animated, and a Deaf child was able to explain that she had received the same comic book. Watching the children integrate and react gave the teacher of the Deaf the most joy (Robinson, 1997, p. 19).

The hearing teacher of the hearing children was selected for the project because she was an excellent teacher, was enthusiastic about the project, and was a naturally expressive person. However, she went into the program with no BSL, no knowledge of deafness, and no training in Deaf issues. Although she had never met a Deaf adult or child, she had a few preconceived ideas of areas she thought might not be easy for Deaf children to learn. These included emotions and feelings because of the signs used to describe them and she said: "mathematical concepts might be difficult" (Robinson, 1997, p. 19).

She and the Deaf BSL tutor were expected to be coteachers laboring alongside each other in group and whole-class work. In the beginning, since the hearing teacher of hearing children knew no BSL, it was difficult for her to communicate. She directly and indirectly learned BSL from the Deaf BSL tutor almost by osmosis. She soon began to use signs in storytelling and in classroom management.

This ability gave her confidence, as she had envisioned a barrier, which was quickly evaporating. She comments, "When the children come in (to school now) they wave to me and sign to me because they know I can sign back" (Robinson, 1997, p. 20).

This teacher reported that BSL was providing a number of advantages for her hearing students. They progressed in reading as a result of BSL. She believes BSL helps students who have trouble concentrating.

Children sometimes dreamily listen, but with [signing without speech] they have got to look or they will not get the message. I think it has helped children who find it very difficult to sit and listen and therefore this is a very important thing to come out of the project. (Robinson, 1997, p. 21)

She was surprised to find how useful BSL was for math, as she had originally believed it might be a difficult area for sign. As the project progressed, math was primarily taught by the Deaf BSL tutor and the children had to look at her because they could not hear her (no speech). This attention helped them concentrate on the visual aspect, and their mathematical achievement and interest increased, much to everyone's delight.

The hearing teacher of hearing students said BSL was more than just a second language as it permeated the entire classroom. If the second language instruction had been French or German, it would normally be taught at only one particular time, but with BSL the second language came into play in classroom control, social skills, geography, math, storytelling, and vocabulary development. BSL became an integral part of the children's language development. The hearing students' teacher stressed that she observed some children using sign to stimulate their memory. In her estimation this memory-provoking attribute of BSL is useful in myriad ways.

The project affected the hearing children in other ways, as well. The use of BSL appeared to increase their enthusiasm for learning; as their teacher put it, "It was lovely to see their keenness" (Robinson, 1997, p. 21). In the social arena, they learned a great deal about children who were deaf and their attitude toward them became positive. Through the interaction in the integrated classroom the hearing children came to know these Deaf children as normal children who happen to be deaf. The hearing teacher of hearing students wanted to emphasize the point that the children see the BSL Deaf tutor as a teacher, not a Deaf person.

The BSL Deaf tutor was chosen for the project because she sees and experiences the world from a Deaf perspective and, by doing so, provides important insights into the integrated classroom. BSL is her first language, written English her second. She was born without hearing and does not speak. Before the start of the program she expected the mainstream school to be lonely, with no one to talk to in her language. She knew from past experience that the hearing staff would be more worried than she was, and she was confident the children would pick up the sign quickly. She was in the hearing classroom for two and one half days each week, two days with just the hearing students and one half day in the integrated setting with both Deaf and hearing children.

The BSL tutor thinks hearing children profit from having a Deaf adult in the classroom, as they learn not only BSL, but also communication with a Deaf person. It is a real-life situation and the children intuitively pick up things, such as Deaf etiquette, ways to gain a Deaf person's attention, and eye contact. This all occurs easily and naturally.

One of the tutor's beliefs before the program began was that the hearing children would develop Sign Supported English (SSE), not BSL. She was wrong; the children developed and used their own sign language structure (the early beginnings of BSL), and some of the children used BSL structure. The tutor feels that the unexpected development of BSL grammar and structure came about because the children did not use their voices, as using their voices forces them to use signs within an English structure. The children instinctively did not use their voices with her, for they could tell it would be a waste of time.

Throughout the project, the teaching covered a lot of national curriculum topics related to food, drink, clothes, countries, weather, math, plus current events. No special time was set aside for learning BSL; it was merged into daily lessons by using vocabulary connected to those lessons. Sign names were given to all students. They loved their new insignias and happily used them with the BSL tutor and the other children.

The children were readily able to communicate with the Deaf BSL tutor about their work through sign language. A few hearing children found it hard to discriminate between two similar signs, and sometimes they could not make a sign because they lacked the flexibility. On such occasions she would substitute other signs for them to use.

The most difficult aspect of teaching the hearing children BSL proved to be eye contact. Eye contact is the basis of a signed language, and it cannot occur without it. Hearing children do not use their eyes as Deaf children do. Their dominant sense is hearing. The BSL tutor relates a story that illustrates the point. She was working with a hearing child in a room where two hearing adults were talking. The student was struggling to understand her (visually) while another (aural) language was being imposed. She recalls that the adults were asked to leave the room because according to the BSL tutor, it is impossible to use or absorb two languages with two different structures at the same time.

The Deaf BSL tutor judges that the hearing children developed a positive attitude toward the Deaf children to some extent through classroom interaction with them, but she believes it primarily occurred because of her presence as a Deaf adult or role model in the classroom. The project was extremely successful for hearing children, and they garnered much from it. She believes that the Deaf children did not benefit to the same extent from the project: "This is not to say that they couldn't benefit if it was thought out and planned properly with Deaf professional input" (Robinson, 1997, pp. 22, 23).

Her wish is to have mainstream schools teach BSL to children without hearing impairments and use BSL with all students at some times during the day. The BSL tutor believes this sort of initiative would help create a learning environment where Deaf students could feel comfortable and confident, because there would be other students and teachers in the school who could understand them and communicate with them in their own language.

In everyone's estimation, at the conclusion of the fourteen-month-long Sign in Education program, the hearing children had gained a good deal. An assessment based on the collated academic evidence showed that instruction in BSL was giving hearing students access to the curriculum, and they were receiving added benefit from its use, as well. Specifically, sign language helped children listen, look, and concentrate. This aptitude to attend expedited concept development. Their reading ability increased, and their English vocabularies were enhanced. Sign aided some youngsters' math growth and in general increased students' enjoyment and motivation (Robinson, 1997, p. 1).

There is no question about the growth of hearing children's BSL skills. They were individually videotaped and tested at the beginning and end of the project. During this BSL assessment the student's task was to describe pictures by using sign language. When the program started, they knew no sign language. Naturally, they had great difficulty communicating the pictures to the interviewer in BSL and did not even attempt to use simple gesture. When the program ended, the children were able to use BSL handshape, placement, and space correctly, albeit at an early level of development. They knew their colors and numbers in BSL. It was estimated from comparing the videos of the hearing and Deaf children that the hearing students were about a year behind the Deaf students in BSL ability at the end of the project (Robinson, 1997, p. 39).

The hearing students' BSL developed through general exposure to the language during the school day. They instinctively absorbed information about deafness, they formed a positive attitude toward Deaf children and adults, they acquired a range of communication skills, and they actively sought to make friendships with the Deaf children. The project was an absolute win-win situation for the hearing children.

On the other hand, the Deaf children appeared to acquire fewer gains from the project. Obviously the "deaf-friendly" environment created in the mainstream school; the BSL usage, which they were better at than their hearing counterparts; and the positive Deaf role model in the person of the Deaf tutor should all serve to heighten their self-confidence, though self-confidence is difficult, if not impossible, to evaluate and assess.

They did have greater access to the national curriculum, particularly storytelling, geography, and math. No specific advancement in their academic abilities in any of these areas was noted or reported. This does not mean that the project was not valuable, just that its benefit could not be determined with precision.

The Deaf children's BSL ability was evaluated in the same manner as the hearing children's. As would be expected, they did far better in their initial evaluation than the hearing children because they knew some BSL. Their concluding videotaped test shows that there was steady improvement in the Deaf students' acquisition of BSL grammar and structure. Their BSL language gains were significant and assessable.

Although it was not noted in the written report, it would seem that the Deaf children should have received some intrinsic benefit from their role as teachers' aides. They helped their hearing classmates form numbers and letters in the manual alphabet, showed them the way to make some signs, and helped them correctly match signs with colors. No emphasis was placed on these activities, which are clearly evident in the videotaped record of the classroom. The incidence of these encounters appears to have increased as the project progressed.

The final example of inclusive education I cover in this chapter is the Newcomb College Nursery School, a Louisiana preschool located on the campus of Tulane University. A few years ago, when the nursery school's coteachers learned that two three-year-olds with hearing impairments would be included in their afternoon classes, they immediately decided to teach the entire class sign language. Neither teacher knew how to sign, but because of their knowledge of young children, they felt this would create the least restrictive educational environment for the children with hearing needs. They also reasoned that it would provide an enriching experience for the children with normal hearing.

The two teachers began taking sign language classes over the summer to prepare for the fall. They planned to integrate sign totally into the curriculum, using it concurrently with spoken English with all of the children at all times. They made no attempts to modify the existing curriculum, and when school started, they proceeded to teach as they had in previous years, except that they added sign language.

They also had meetings with the parents to allay any fears that the inclusive educational program would negatively impact the language development of the typical students. These forums gave them an opportunity to explain the endeavor more fully and to demonstrate some signing as well. Regular newsletters and parent-teacher conferences continued to keep the parents abreast of the bilingual approach.

These exchanges soon became a two-way street, as the teachers learned that the students were teaching their parents how to sign at home. This did not surprise them as the children had taken to the signing in an easy and natural way, rapidly catching on and effortlessly copying the teachers' finger movements and handshapes. Both teachers also realized that signing had additional personal benefits, as they silently communicated with each other via sign far across the playground or at a distance in the classroom.

At the end of the first year, the teachers and the parents were pleased with the outcome of the full inclusion. It seemed that word of the program's success was spreading and that other students from the community with hearing impairments would be enrolled in the nursery school. They had not originally conceived this as a research program but determined that they had a golden opportunity to collect data and actually study the academic advantage of bilingual instruction.

A university researcher was added to the team to design a two-year pilot study. The research question they hoped to answer was, What is the effect of using signing on the receptive English vocabulary of middle-class preschoolers who have normal hearing and language development? (Heller, Manning, Pavur, & Wagner, 1998, p. 51).

There were fifty-four student participants in the study, who constituted four three-year-old classes. The signing cohort consisted of twenty-nine children with normal hearing who were taught sign, and the nonsigning cohort consisted of twenty-five children who were not taught sign. In all other respects the same curriculum was used in both classes. A 1:7 teacher-to-student ratio was maintained throughout the research, and at least one teacher in each of the classes changed during the period of the study. This made it less likely that the impact of one particular teacher could skew the results.

They measured the students' vocabulary with a pre- and posttest design, selecting the Peabody Picture Vocabulary Test (PPVT-R) as their testing instrument, as I had in my research in Maryland. The outcome of this endeavor was much the same as I had found on my earlier studies:

When sign language instruction was integrated in a naturalistic way into the general preschool curriculum, both hearing and nonhearing children benefited. After 1 year in an inclusive signing classroom, children without hearing impairments had language development superior to that of their peers. All children profited cognitively when they used signing in a natural setting to communicate with each other. (Heller et al., 1998, p. 52)

This study shows that the benefits of full inclusion go well beyond social and emotional advantages. Signing presents preschoolers with a measurable cognitive advantage that is statistically significant. In addition to this finding, the teachers in this preschool project stressed that from the first day of school the children's enthusiasm never waned, their hands were constantly flying, and they were involved in a positive way in their education. They also report a social advantage that echoes the experience of the British project. Since including sign language, the students express less frustration, are more congenial, and have far fewer conflicts in the classroom. Pupils are engaged, and they remain enthusiastic and eager to learn. Teachers attribute the pleasant environment to the unique communication property they feel sign offers the students.

All the evidence gathered from the three inclusive programs featured in this chapter—the multigraded Alaskan endeavor, the pilot project in the United Kingdom, and the preschool initiative at Tulane University—shows that sign language instruction in the hearing classroom provides an educational advantage for hearing children: Including sign language in the curriculum improves their vocabulary, reading, spelling, and math. Sign helps children focus, concentrate, and remember. It generates enthusiasm for learning, is an effective and appropriate aid in classroom management, and has been shown to lessen conflict, ease tension, and contribute to a harmonious learning environment.

An additional advantage, which may be more fully appreciated by some of the hearing children in time, is that when young English-speaking children learn sign they have begun to learn another language and are on the path to bilingualism. This early knowledge of sign language, albeit in the initial stages of acquisition, could prove to be useful to those youngsters who select sign language as their "foreign" language choice in high school or college. Other students whose interest has been piqued may independently proceed on the bilingual road and continue to learn sign. When they grow up and enter the work force, in many professions their signing knowledge will benefit them. For instance, bilingual medical professionals earn higher salaries and are in far greater demand than those proficient in only one language.

To date there is a meager amount of documented evidence supporting the academic value of inclusion for children who are Deaf. This is not unusual at this point, because the instances of full inclusion for Deaf children have been rare, as heretofore most of these primary age children have been educated in residential schools for the Deaf. Although neither the academic achievement nor the social development of Deaf children educated in mainstream classrooms is well documented at this time, it would only seem to make common sense that educating their hearing peers to communicate with them in ASL would ultimately prove to be advantageous for them.

REFERENCES

Heller, I., Manning, D., Pavur, D., & Wagner, K. (1998). Let's all sign! Enhancing language development in an inclusive preschool. *Teaching Exceptional Children*, Jan/Feb, 50–53.

Robinson, K. (1997). *Sign in education: The teaching of hearing children British Sign Language in school*. Birmingham, England: Teesside Tec.

PART III
Theory

_____ Chapter 9 _____

Why It Works

When people learn about using sign language to enhance hearing children's education, they express interest and usually accept the evidence offered that it works. Without fail, the first question always asked is, Why? Why is sign effective? This chapter attempts to answer the question. I start with some of the facts that are known, move to an area that remains theoretical at this time, and conclude with reasons that reside in the realm of speculation. You will find more sources cited in this chapter than in the rest of the book. In the context of this material they are necessary, but I have tried to keep them to a minimum.

Before I start, it is important to have some background and understanding of sign language. The reasoning that follows is based on the ideas discussed in Chapter 2 on sign language. Always remember that in American Sign Language (ASL), sign uses gesture in the same way that American English speech uses sound. An ASL sign is more than a gesture, in the same way that an English word is more than a sound: An individual sign is a unit of the language known as ASL; an individual word is a unit of the language known as English. ASL and English are distinct languages. This distinction brings us to the first explanation of the positive effect of sign language on hearing children's education.

KNOWN FACTS

Memory

Memory is related to language storage and retrieval. How do people locate their language; how do they find and use their alphabet, their words? It is known that languages are stored in the left hemisphere of the brain. In 1963, Kolers suggested that different languages use different memory stores. Since his original research on the topic his findings have been tested repeatedly by other investigators concerned with understanding language. The two languages used in many of these linguistic studies were English and Spanish. One such study, published by J. Goggin and D. Wickens in 1971, showed that separate language stores were established in the left hemisphere of the brain for persons who were unequally fluent in two spoken languages, English and Spanish. Goggin and Wickens's results supported Kolers's hypothesis that individuals have a separate language memory store for each of their spoken languages.

Before William Stokoe's pioneering work, *Sign Language Structures* (1960), sign language was viewed either as a system of gestures or as an inferior manual form of English. Stokoe's discoveries gave ASL linguistic status, providing the support for the conceptualization of ASL as a structured language with unique grammar, syntax, and morphology. When considered in that light, sign language became appropriate fodder for further linguistic study.

In 1978, Hoemann conducted the first investigation of sign language and memory stores. He endeavored to determine whether the previous findings concerning spoken languages and memory would hold true in the case of a signed language like ASL. What effect, if any, would the difference in modality from a spoken language to a signed language have on language and memory stores? Would a learners' ASL be located in a separate memory store from their English, as are two spoken languages such as English and Spanish?

This is the question Hoemann set out to answer in his research concerning ASL and English. The subjects in his first study were students from Gallaudet University. In a second study, he went on to use upper and middle school pupils in a residential school for the deaf. Both groups of subjects demonstrated that there was an individual memory store for each language. ASL had a memory store and English had a memory store.

Over the ensuing years Hoemann continued to investigate this area of interest. He published another study on the topic with Koenig in 1990. In this study, conducted at Bowling Green State University, in Ohio, the subjects were ninety-six English-speaking college students enrolled in an ASL course. At the time of the testing, they had from three to five weeks of experience with ASL and the manual alphabet. The results they obtained establish that hearing English-speaking persons, learning ASL as a second language, employ two separate memory stores.

The data gathered in this study confirm the conclusion that one individual memory store houses the manual alphabet and ASL, and another houses the English alphabet characters and English. These outcomes are a clear replication of the results of the earlier research studies conducted by Goggin and Wickens as well as Hoemann's own initial studies with ASL. The research supports the generalization of this finding to hearing persons who are just beginning to learn ASL. It can therefore be concluded that all languages, whether spoken or signed, are categorically coded and housed in distinct memory stores even in the earliest stages of their acquisition.

Now what does this fact about separate memory stores mean to us when we are trying to discover why ASL is working? Could the reason sign language helps hearing English-speaking children learn how to read, or remember how to spell a word, or actually increase their English vocabulary be that they are now learning a new language and with this new language they have acquired a new memory store? Undoubtedly, because of ASL's linguistic status, this is the case.

As a result of the way the human brain stores all languages, the young student learning a new language has two places to look for the information. Even in the initial days of sign language instruction, this separate memory store where the child can locate answers exists. It is a new storehouse for information providing youngsters with an additional data base that they can access easily and quickly. If they do not find the answer in their English data base, they may find it in their ASL data base.

Their language center located in the left hemisphere of the brain allows them to flip effortlessly between the two sources to find the ASL sign that will support the written English word, or the manual alphabetic letter that reminds them how to spell an English word, or the ASL sign that provides the clue to the meaning of the English word. The preceding examples illustrate how sign language helps hearing children with reading, spelling, and vocabulary. ASL is able to aid children's memory with its autonomous memory store by creating a built-in redundancy that establishes two independent language sources for children to use for search and recall.

Growth

Recent scholarship has examined brain growth and development. Research indicates that the left cerebral hemisphere, with its innate predisposition for the central components of language, independently of language modality, needs language activity to form physically and to develop. Rymer writes, "Language is a logic system so organically tuned to the mechanism of the human brain that it actually triggers the brain's growth" (1992, p. 69). It has been shown that brain development itself is responsive to the reception of language.

Sign language instruction, with its requisite visual component, creates an increase in brain activity by engaging the visual cortex and presenting an additional language to the young learner. The heightened cerebral action occurs in both the right and left hemispheres of the brain. This increase in language activity stimulates the development of the brain by stimulating the formation of more synapses, or connections among brain cells. The brains of children up to about the age of eight continue to develop and grow in this manner, in response to environmental input. Brain cells literally live or die as language experiences impinge upon them. Using sign language and English in tandem provides a much richer language base for brain activity and brain growth and development.

Visual

The visual aspect is closely linked to the two aspects already discussed. Sign training and use rely heavily on sight, which is directly related to a child's development. More than half of the brain is devoted to visual processing. In fact, even though articulated language production and internal processing are developing in young children, they are taking most of their behavioral cues from what they see, not from spoken instructions. Just think of the way children respond to a "look" given by a parent or a teacher.

This reliance on the brain's visual cortex, which begins in infancy, is maintained even in adulthood, when, research indicates, 65 percent of the content in two-person communication is transmitted in the nonverbal channel through body language (Mehrabian, 1981). Recent findings reported by Goleman (1995) show that seeing stimulates the formation of increasingly complex neural circuitry in the brain. During the first six years of life the eyes are more acute receptors of knowledge and vision itself produces a measurable impact on the developing visual cortex.

This finding corroborates extensive studies conducted by Bonvillian and Floven (1993), who found that both motor ability and visual perception account for the ease and speed of sign language acquisition in young children. At birth, the level of maturation of the motor centers is ahead of that of the speech centers; this differential level is maintained during early development and continues in childhood. Basic motor control of the hands occurs before control of the voice and speech, and the visual cortex matures before the auditory cortex. These factors led Bellugi et al. (1994) to conclude that linguistic functioning in a visual medium both requires and results in greater visuospatial processing abilities.

Studies of the way children acquire spoken languages have shown their natural propensity for linguistic analysis at a generally subconscious level. Because sign language is visual-gestural language, you might think it is acquired in a radically different way than a spoken language is acquired. This is not the case. In fact, the acquisition process is remarkably similar in both. The critical difference lies in the visual-spatial nature of sign language. This visual component triggers a stronger involvement of the right hemisphere of the brain as it deals with sign language perception and processing.

The eyes are the receptors for ASL as the ears are the receptors for English. Language, however, is not limited to its receptors, to the eyes or the ears. How is the brain organized to process language delivered in a visual modality? Research on ASL shows sign is perceived in a visuospatial manner by the right hemisphere of the brain and subsequently processed by the left hemisphere. Analysis of the patterns of breakdown of a visuospatial language in deaf signers, reported in *What the Hands Reveal about the Brain* (Poizner et al., 1987), provides a further perspective on cerebral specialization for languages. Although the case studies show that the left hemisphere is dominant for language whether the language is signed or spoken, individual cases indicate that there is a right hemisphere specialization for visuospatial functioning.

The involvement of the right brain is the aspect that defines sign language and sets it apart from all spoken languages. Although the left hemisphere has the dominant role in the final processing of all languages, including sign, it is the right hemisphere that is dominant for the initial intake and processing of visuospatial relationships in sign language. The specialization of the right hemisphere is a particularly important characteristic of sign language because children in general, and special populations of children in particular, garner significant benefit from a greater involvement with visual learning.

To understand a word the learner must invoke a visual image of that word in the mind's eye. If students cannot access underlying images for the words within their own minds, the words will remain incomprehensible to them. When teachers use sign language with children the meaning of the word is often present and transmitted within the sign itself, as a result of signs' iconic nature. When a sign is not iconic, it still offers a visual picture for the word. In either case, whether iconic or not, sign language provides a visual image from which learning can occur.

A special population of children receiving definite benefit from more opportunities to engage in visual learning are children diagnosed with attention deficit disorder (ADD). The point is clearly articulated by Freed and Parsons in *Right-Brained Children in a Left-Brained World: Unlocking the Potential of Your ADD Child*: "It is a given that these youngsters (ADD) must visualize in order to learn and that they process exclusively in pictures" (1997, p. 61). By tapping into the proclivity and need of such children to visualize, the use of sign language increases the potential learning occasions for these visual learners.

It is also true that another type of child with a visual learning style who can be particularly helped with sign language is the child with dyslexia. Children who have this condition are known to need to make mental pictures as they read. When these youngsters are trying to learn to read, words that have no pictures, for example, *the* or *then*, wipe their mental blackboard clean (Davis & Braun, 1997). Sign gives such children wonderful pictures for words, pictures that they are able both to see and to feel. Receiving and producing signs can provide a decided advantage for these students.

I present a final point in this section pertaining to the advantage offered by sign language's visual aspect for both typical children and special populations in regard to their ability to learn how to read. The visual action described relates to human beings in general, but it provides particular benefits for children. Research has shown that our visual sense functions most effectively when our eyes are actively moving. When the eyes stop moving we lose sensory information because the external eye muscles no longer move up and down or side to side, or all around; therefore, our processing is limited to internal brain function. This is what happens when you stare. However, in an active learning situation, the eyes are constantly moving. Perceiving, processing, or producing sign language would be an active learning situation that would trigger accompanying eye movement. The more the eyes move, the more the muscles of both eyes will work together. This action provokes brain growth. As the eye muscles strengthen and move in concert with each other, additional connections to the brain develop and become available. The result is efficient eye teaming, which enables the student to focus, track, and concentrate when reading (Hannaford, 1995).

Movement

Movement relates to the message as it is kinesthetically produced by the child, not to the previously cited movement of the eyes. Piaget stated, "Gesture and mime—language in movement is the real social language of the child" (1955, p. 77). If one concurs with Piaget's perspective that language and movement are native to the child, a position supported by recent scholars, then ASL, which is indeed language in movement, should provide a more natural mode for children's language acquisition and development than English. Further justification for Piaget's position is provided in the research advanced by Newport and Meir (1985, Meir, 1991), which found that signs are more easily understood by young children than spoken words.

Piaget (1976) also claims that thinking and learning are anchored by movement. In the absence of movement you do not have conscious thought, and without conscious thought you are deprived of meaning. Many other outstanding specialists in the field of learning such as Maria Montessori and Paul Dennison, who said, "Movement is the door to learning," concur with Piaget and espouse the importance of movement to the learning process. Often adults anchor or pin down a thought with movement by making written notes. Young children's writing skills are inadequate for such note taking. Sign language can give children a medium through which they can use the movement of the sign itself, as they produce it, to anchor their own thought. The action of producing the sign generates thought and meaning. Each sign with its accompanying movement becomes a vital link in thought processing and learning.

Furthermore, in this same vein, the manual alphabet associated with sign language provides an easy, convenient form of writing for young children. Children can fingerspell much sooner than they acquire the manual dexterity to write words with pencil on paper. Thomas Hopkins Gallaudet, the pioneer of education for the deaf in the United States, advocated that hearing siblings of deaf children learn and use the manual alphabet and signs because he was convinced it would assist hearing children's language acquisition. He also believed fingerspelling familiarized children with correct orthography at an early age. In an 1853 issue of the *American Annals of the Deaf,* which happens to be the oldest academic journal published in the United States, Bartlett, recounting Gallaudet's earlier assertion concerning the value of sign for hearing children, describes the principles on which he believes Gallaudet based his convictions: "The more varied the form under which language is presented to the mind through the various senses, the more perfect will be the knowledge of it acquired, and the more permanently will it be retained" (1853, p. 33).

Another interesting element that ties into the movement aspect is that Broca's area of the frontal lobe controls skillful movements of the hands, the kind of movements used to produce sign language or letters from the manual alphabet. This is the same area of the brain that controls inner speech. Inner speech plays a significant role in the way we process information and think. It develops naturally in human beings, gradually increasing in an incremental manner as they mature. We evaluate data and promote contemplation through the medium of inner speech at a much faster rate and in a more efficient manner than would be possible with verbalization. This internal processing establishes language patterns that correspond to inner images and gestures.

Because inner speech and adept hand movements are managed by the same area of the brain, when sign language is employed, there is an increased opportunity for the formation of a greater number of connections and patterns in the brain. Both the small movements of the fingers and hands and the larger movement of the arms and body associated with the construction and delivery of communication via sign language have a particular advantage for developing children. Hannaford succinctly expresses the point concerning the value of movement: "Movement is an indispensable part of learning and thinking. Each movement becomes a vital link to learning and thought processing. . . . Movement is an integral part of all mental processing" (1997, p. 107).

Meaning

When children are learning to read, they must make some sense of the combination of letters that form a word. For optimal word recognition and comprehension, children must associate the characters on a page with a concrete idea or image in their mind. Grasping something new, particularly at this young age, is best achieved by making connections, by anchoring the word on the page to something familiar. If the word on the page can be tied to an internal image or emotion, understanding it is easier. Aristotle crystallized this idea for his students in ancient Greece when he wrote, "The soul never thinks without a picture."

This fact was recently demonstrated in a study at the University of Toronto (Tulving, et al., 1994). Position emission tomographic (PET) scans showed that participants had a far stronger recall and recognition for words analyzed by meaning, as compared to words pursued on a letter-by-letter basis. To learn something new most effectively, it is best to unite it with an existing sensory, emotional, or physical event. Personally experienced episodes or known objects and people are the templates children use for acquiring the meaning of words.

Sign language, because of its iconic nature, readily signals the meaning of words to children and aids the process of tying the written word to an internal remembered image. Signs' transparency transmits an external picture that is instantly and effortlessly transformed into an internal picture. The facsimile provided by the sign triggers a concrete idea or image in the child's mind. For the young child who is learning to read, this process establishes the word's meaning and serves to hook this meaning to memory. Forming cerebral associations with the written word is the basis of reading.

Play

When children use sign language they become more actively involved in play. This appears to transpire as a result of their increased understanding and use of symbols. Through this dynamic association with symbols, the students' facility for play is apparently stimulated. Research findings show that sign language has a unique proclivity for inspiring play activity, as children relate to the symbols embedded in its grammar as the toys of play. Increasing a child's capacity for play, as well as increasing the amount of time a child is involved in the activity of play, can have a significant influence on their development.

The importance of childhood play and its interdependence with learning and growth has been recognized since the Russian developmental psychologist Lev Vygotsky (1962, 1978) proposed that play should dominate the "zone of proximal development" (ZPD). His theory was an attempt to explain consciousness as the product of socialization. Most of his original work was done in the context of language learning in children.

Vygotsky (1978, p. 56) gives the example of pointing a finger. Initially this behavior begins as a meaningless grasping motion; however, as people around the baby or child react to the gesture, it becomes a movement that has meaning. In particular the pointing gesture represents an interpersonal connection between individuals. A child's first utterances with peers or adults are done for the purpose of communication, but once mastered they become internalized and allow "inner speech."

The major theme of Vygotsky's theoretical framework is that social interaction plays a fundamental role in the development of cognition. The potential for full development is limited to the particular time span he refers to as the ZPD. For Vygotsky play was the centerpiece of the ZPD as it constituted an integral and essential part of learning and development. He viewed play, in its connection to learning and development, as a simultaneous question and answer conception of activity, explaining that learning and development do not have a cause-and-effect relationship but rather coexist and complete each other, in a coexisting reciprocal relationship.

This perspective that play and learning have a symbiotic relationship is apparent in the position of contemporary developmental psychologists who accept the capacity to play as a cause, as well as a correlate, of cognition, social growth, and language ability. During play a consolidation of skills occurs and is carried over to contexts beyond those in which they are obtained. A lack of competence or comfort with language alters children's interactive experiences and decreases the degree to which they can learn from play.

According to other studies cited by Spencer and Deyo (1993), hearing children with language difficulties suffer from an underlying pervasive symbolic deficit. Such children, often labeled language-delayed or language-disordered, have accompanying delays in symbolic play despite otherwise normal cognitive functioning. Using sign language with hearing children enhances their capacity for play by augmenting or increasing their understanding and use of symbols. Characteristically, this enhancement of play activity leads to a corresponding development of language, both sign language and English.

Hand

Sign language relies on the use of the hand to a degree not present when one is communicating with English. When speaking English, or reading English, or listening to English, it is not necessary to engage the hand and the hand is seldom involved. The hand is only necessary when English is being written. Children, particularly young children, spend very little time writing. At first they do not know how to write or print and need to be taught. This is a laborious, unnatural process for them. On the other hand, no pun intended, using their hands is natural, and children effortlessly use their hands for comfort, communication, and acquisition of information from the time of their birth.

When you observe babies you can see them experiment with their hands. They move them about; they touch their hands together; they try to reach things; they attempt to pick up objects. The information they garner in this manner is written in the tactile kinesthetic language of manipulation and movement. It is returned to the brain and compared with the information from the visual system, as part of a process through which the brain creates visuospatial images. Through this interaction between the brain and the hand a kind of dual learning takes place. As the late Canadian author Robertson Davies (1986, p. 88) wrote, "The hand speaks to the brain as surely as the brain speaks to the hand."

In Wilson's treatise *The Hand: How Its Use Shapes the Brain, Language and Human Culture* (1998), he credits the work of the nineteenth-century Scottish surgeon and anatomy teacher Sir Charles Bell as much of his inspiration. Bell's insight into the interconnected relationships among movement, perception, and learning was revolutionary in his own time. He stressed the interdependence of hand and brain function. According to Bell, both the hand and eye develop as sense organs through practice, as the brain teaches itself by making the hand and eye learn to work together. The brain constructs images based on the messages received from the eye and the hand. It records a collection of sensory data derived from eye and limb movements. As we move into the twenty-first century, contemporary research bears out and strengthens Bell's nineteenth-century assertions concerning the coupling of hand and eye movement and the relationship of this process to the emergence of thought and language development.

Wilson, a neurologist at the University of California School of Medicine in San Francisco, emphasizes the point that the thought-language nexus becomes a hand-thought-language nexus. The child learns with real objects unified through a sequence of actions organizing a child's active movements and sensorimotor explorations. However, Wilson stresses that "none of the neurophysiological brain activity can be related to real language until it gains access to an input-output channel: in-the-body sensorimotor system for detecting external events and generating bodily responses" (p. 188).

Sign language is eminently suited to serve as the input-output channel. When connections among interwoven strands of language and thought are created with sign language, language and thought are intrinsically attached to what is happening to the child's hand. As the brain learns to send and receive coded messages, language milestones occur in concert with motor milestones, developing on parallel tracks, but always interconnected, interdependent, growing, reinforcing, and influencing each other. The hand is the biomechanical link found at the end or the beginning, depending on your perspective, of an elaborate, enormously complex physical and mental circuit. The brain is uniquely suited and prepared to assimilate the plethora of visuospatial information that it receives as a result of the intercourse between hand and brain. Sign language has a unique capacity to tap into the natural exchange between hand and brain, optimizing the emergence of language in the child because of the physiological advantage ASL presents over English.

Summary

In each of the components cited I have tried to identify exactly what is transpiring in order to illustrate why sign language gives hearing students a linguistic advantage. Separating the various aspects into

individual categories is helpful for understanding the distinct operations involved in the process, but it also creates an artificial picture.
In actuality, a cohesive interrelatedness exists among all of the aspects
discussed. For example, memory is connected to growth and relies
on visual, movement, meaning, play, and of course manual stimuli.
If all of the other elements were not actively involved in the process
there would be nothing generated to place, or retain, in the separate
sign language memory store located in the left hemisphere of the
brain.

All the attributes cited are responsible for the positive effect of sign
language on children's literacy. The various components working together create an educational advantage for hearing children. In the
next section I examine an area that I believe to be relevant to the
processes at work when sign language is incorporated in hearing children's education but where questions remain.

AREA OF THEORY

Origins of Language

Although there is not complete agreement concerning the origins
and operations of language, there is no dispute that Broca's area of
the left hemisphere is specialized for language processing. Furthermore, it is widely believed that this neural infrastructure for language
must have been in place for a long time, and in the parlance of linguists, this infrastructure would be preadapted to include two basic
requirements of language: the arbitrariness of sign and a discrete combinational system.

Human beings appear to have acquired a natural proclivity for sign
and gesture in the course of their development. On an evolutionary
time scale, when the forelimbs were freed of the obligation to support
body weight, the hand and the brain met and began to create language, thereby redefining the demands and possibilities of life. This
concept is fully explored in Corballis's article "The Gestural Origins
of Language" in *American Scientist* (1999).

Corballis believes recent findings on how chimpanzees and deaf
babies communicate with hand gestures provide an answer to one of
the key mysteries of human evolution. His position supports the idea
first postulated by the seventeenth-century French philosopher
Etienne Condillac that human language emerged not from vocaliza-

tion, but from manual gestures. Scientific discoveries suggest that the change from a gestural to a vocal mode occurred quite recently in humanoid evolution with the emergence of *Homo sapiens* in Africa a mere 150,000 or so years ago.

Early humanoids would have been vulnerable to other species, and gestural communication, because it is silent and spatial, would be more suited to their communication needs for stealth and illustration. Gestural language has an iconic character that illustrates the shape and position of objects or action in space. Corballis points out that if the earliest languages were gestural, that characteristic would help to explain how words arbitrarily came to represent objects and actions: "What may have begun as an iconic system could plausibly have evolved more abstract properties over time, and at some point arbitrary patterns of sound may have been linked to gestures that may themselves have become abstract symbols rather than icons" (p. 141).

William C. Stokoe, who recognized that sign language was indeed a language (p. 77, chap. 6), does not see the full language legitimacy he and others helped bestow on ASL as his greatest accomplishment. Rather, he explains:

> What I consider my principal discovery is how language must have begun as Sign. That is to say briefly: an upright walking visually oriented, late evolving primate species began to see that body movements really did mean what they looked as if they meant. Voices can make sound but the only way that a wealth of meanings can be connected to sounds is by being told what the sounds mean. If gestures had developed into actual language—and much sign research shows they have done so; then sounds habitually uttered along with gestures would have become connected with the meanings that the gestures had naturally signified. (Stokoe, 1996, p. 388)

Stokoe's words mirror Corballis's position, and both support the view that language evolved from hand to mouth. Recognizing sign language as the precursor of spoken language accounts for the early physiological preference gesture held as a communication channel. Nature appears to bestow an early bias for sign language production, indicated by the close functional link existing between speech and sign. This engenders sign with an intrinsic natural capacity for language delivery. This component remains in the area of developmental theory, but recent scientific discoveries may confirm the gestural origins of language. If this does occur, it will provide yet another rationale, however tangential, for understanding the significance of sign, as it would appear that sign is embedded in the evolutionary history of human beings.

REALM OF SPECULATION

In this section I cover a number of additional advantages sign language appears to provide for hearing students. Some actually contribute to our understanding of why sign works, and others relate to educational enrichment in general. At this time, they are in the realm of speculation and undoubtedly will remain there, as these benefits are difficult to identify clearly without accompanying confounders and are generally impossible to measure or assess. The advantages considered here are children's ability to attend, self-esteem, and enthusiasm for learning, and the educational enrichment that classroom climate, second language acquisition, and cultural awareness can produce.

Attend

The capacity to attend is interesting because there is something of a dichotomy in children's makeup. We all have observed children who are so clearly focused on an object such as a kite or a bird that they track it with complete absorption. I recall my grandchild's being so taken with a hot air balloon that he followed it, running across a golf course in Vermont, gleefully repeating, "Balloon, balloon." As he scurried along, it was difficult to dissuade him from his pursuit even when he encountered a stream. It was as if he had become one with the object.

On the other hand, as far as the behavior of children is concerned, this same level of interest does not often exist in the classroom. Often teachers are presented with the task of engaging their students in learning activities. This is not as simple as the example of my grandson and the balloon. Sign language presents an advantage in this realm. Children demonstrate a natural curiosity and interest in learning sign without any prodding or pushing. As they sign, they become active participants in learning. Young people express a great deal of pleasure as they create visual symbols that represent words. They actually look forward to it and enjoy it. Sign language is engaging for children.

When a teacher is speaking, the students do not have to look at the teacher to receive the message. However, teachers find students gain more from the instruction if they do look at the instructor and do not let their eyes wander all over the room. Therefore, teachers are constantly struggling to get students to pay attention and focus their eyes on the lesson at hand. When the teacher is using sign language, there is no struggle. The nature or properties of the language itself force the students to keep their eyes on the teacher. Pupils focus, concentrate, and pay attention. Teachers find this aspect of sign language to be a great advantage.

Self Esteem

Using sign language may increase some students' self-esteem. This of course is a difficult aspect to measure, but teachers who use sign in their classes report that their students display more pride, heightened stature, and greater competence in interpersonal communication. Sign benefits all students, but in terms of results of vocabulary and reading evaluations, it tends to provide a larger boost to the more needy student. Students are actually doing better academically, and this improvement may very well account for their increased self-esteem.

Enthusiasm

When students begin to learn sign language, they become more interested and engaged in their schoolwork. After learning sign language they express added pleasure in communicating. It is different: They know something a lot of "big people" don't know. It is a secret code that they can use with their friends. They like to teach their families the signs, so that they can communicate with them in this new language. Because it is a legitimate foreign language it has credibility. They routinely see people using it on television, when interpreters in small circles sign important speeches or worship services. They see sign in commercials, and they are able to understand the sign and excitedly report this to their teachers. Sign is fun and they like it.

Enrichment

Sign language changes the classroom climate. It is quieter. The teacher signs the management phrases such as *sit down, line up*, and *wash your hands*. There is none of the paralanguage of annoyance that sometimes creeps into teachers' voices when they are forced to repeat the same phrases again and again or have to deal with a child who needs more direction. Children respond more readily to signs than they do to spoken instructions—perhaps because it is different, maybe because it has that secret code thing going for it. It is unclear just why, but all teachers who have used it report that the students like it and react quickly to directions given in sign.

They also have found that there is less conflict in the classroom as children use their signs to express their feelings and rarely resort to pushing or hitting classmates. The class is a more mellow place. As one teacher put it: "All of these children are totally detached; they come from noise and media talk, and video games and electronic communication. Sign quiets them and calms them. It redirects them and they learn how to talk together to each other with their hands."

Sign language enriches a child's education. It presents a foreign language in an easily accessible manner. When a second language is introduced to a child at an early age, it is more likely to be learned and retained. As sign now fulfills foreign language requirements in an increasing number of high schools and most colleges in this country, the child who begins to learn it in elementary school gains an academic advantage.

With the language children are introduced to a culture as well. They will learn about and come to understand people who are deaf. They should be able to communicate with them. And undoubtedly they will have opportunities to do just this in their own schools. In a day and age when, as a result of the Americans with Disabilities Act (ADA), inclusion is the law of the land, this is almost inevitable. Deaf culture is rich and interesting and children who are exposed to it from a tender age will reap rewards from this cultural awareness.

CONCLUSION

In this chapter, I have attempted to isolate the individual components of the language acquisition process to provide a keener understanding of the reasons for the positive effect of sign language on hearing children's English literacy. The material has been considered in three broad areas that set forth the rationale for sign use with hearing children: known facts, area of theory, and realm of speculation. You can garner a magnified picture of a portion of the process by viewing each area as an individual entity.

After reading the Known Facts section, which includes memory, visual, meaning, play, hand, and growth aspects, to determine why signing contributes to children's language growth and development, you should readily see how these individual components are all interconnected. Separating them presents a clearer view of what transpires in each component, but it also presents a distorted picture of the process in toto.

Language in its various forms is really all brain stuff. By involving additional parts of the body, such as the eyes, the fingers, the hands, and the arms, in reality you are affecting and influencing the brain itself. The movements that children see and feel, if they are constructing a sign, are occurring as a response to a signal from the brain. In turn, the visual cortex and all of the small movements of the hand and fingers serve to heighten brain activity, the very activity of learning that actually leads to structural alterations in the brain (Kandel, 1991, pp. 1024–1025). Sign language works in a synergetic fashion helping the brain to grow.

According to the neurologist Oliver Sacks (1995, p. xvii), the brain is not programmed and static; rather, it is dynamic and active, a supremely adaptive system geared for evolution and change, needing above all to construct a coherent self and world. The brain is minutely differentiated, with hundreds of tiny areas crucial for every aspect of perception, movement, memory, and language. The miracle is that all these distinct areas cooperate and are integrated in the creation of a self that understands and produces language in a variety of modes.

An apt analogy to end this section would be to compare the human brain to a computer that is hard-wired for language learning. This is a really great computer using the latest Intel processor and Microsoft operating system. It has lots of memory and storage capacity. When presented with only English it does just fine and works well, as if the only program running on it were Microsoft Word. However, when you present the brain with sign language, it is as if your computer were running Microsoft Word with a 20-gigabyte thesaurus, plus a library of thousands of digital images that tie to each word phrase or sentence. The computer would have an immense vocabulary that would be indexed much as a search on the Internet is. It would have more memory and storage, making it capable of performing complex operations with greater speed. In essence, it would be a bigger, better computer. This is akin to what happens to the human brain when it is presented with sign language.

All language whether sign or spoken is not eye stuff, or mouth stuff, or ear stuff; it is brain stuff. But the brain depends on movement, and the brain needs vision, and the brain creates meaning, and the brain relies on memory, and the brain interacts with the hand, and the brain uses play; when sign language is employed with children, as a result of all the overlapping integrated brain activities, the language center of the brain actually grows. This is why sign language works.

In the section on theory I have considered some interesting new scholarship concerning the origins of language that suggests that sign language may well have been the precursor of spoken language. If this is true, it would mean human beings have a powerful physiological base for using sign language. This helps to explain children's comfort and ease with the language.

Finally, in the realm of speculation we have looked at a number of additional advantages sign language provides for hearing children. It influences a child's ability to attend; often increases self-esteem; boosts enthusiasm and readiness to learn; decreases classroom conflict, and generates a quieter, calmer classroom; introduces a foreign language; and raises cultural awareness. All in all, sign language clearly carries educational advantages for hearing children that go far beyond merely improving their literacy.

REFERENCES

Bartlett, D. E. (1853). Family education for young deaf-mute children. *American Annals of the Deaf, 5*, 32–35.

Bellugi, U., O'Grady, L., Lillo-Martin, D., O'Grady Hynes, M., van Hoek, K., & Corina, D. (1994). Enhancement of spatial cognition in deaf children. In V. Volterra & C. J. Erting (Eds.), *From gesture to language in hearing and deaf children* (pp. 278–298). Washington, DC: Gallaudet University Press.

Bonvillian, J. D., & Floven, R. J. (1993). Sign language acquisition: Developmental aspects. In M. Marshark & M. D. Clark (Eds.), *Psychological perspectives on deafness* (pp. 229–265). Hillsdale, NJ: Lawrence Erlbaum Associates.

Corballis, M. C. (1999). The gestural origins of language. *American Scientist, 87*, 138–145.

Davies, R. (1986). *What's bred in the bone.* New York: Penquin Books.

Davis, R., & Braun, E. (1997). *The gift of dyslexia: Why some of the smartest people can't read and how they can learn.* New York: Perigree.

Freed, J., & Parsons, L. (1997). *Right-brained children in a left-brained world: Unlocking the potential of your ADD child.* New York: Simon & Schuster.

Goggin, J., & Wickens D. (1971). Proactive interference and language change in short-term memory. *Journal of Verbal Learning and Verbal Behavior, 10,* 453–458.

Goleman, D. (1995). *Emotional intelligence.* New York: Bantam Books.

Hannaford, C. H. (1995). *Smart moves: Why Learning is not all in your head.* Alexandria, VA: Great Ocean Publishers.

Hoemann, H. (1978). Categorical coding of Sign and English in short term memory by deaf and hearing subjects. In P. A. Siple (Ed.), *Understanding language through Sign Language Research.* New York: Academic Press.

Hoemann, H., & Koenig, T. (1990). Categorical coding of manual and English alphabet characters by beginning students of American Sign Language. *Sign Language Studies, 67,* 175–181.

Kandel, E. (1991). *The Principles of neuroscience* (3rd ed.). New York: Elsevier Press.

Kolers, P. (1963). Interlingual word associations. *Journal of Verbal Learning and Verbal Behavior, 2,* 291–300.

Mehrabian, A. (1981). *Silent messages* (2nd ed.). Belmont, CA: Wadsworth.

Meir, R. P. (1991). Language acquisition by deaf children. *American Scientist, 79,* 60–70.

Newport, E. L., & Meir, R. P. (1985). The acquisition of American Sign Language. In D. I. Solbin (Ed.), *The crosslinguistic study of language acquisition.* Vol. 1: *The data* (pp. 881–938). Hillsdale, NJ: Lawrence Erlbaum Associates.

Piaget, J. (1955). *Language and thought of the child.* New York: Meridian.

Piaget, J. (1976). In S. F. Campbell (Ed.), *Piaget sampler, an introduction to Jean Piaget through his own words* (pp. 15–16, 71–78). New York: Wiley.

Poizner, H., Kilma, E., & Bellugi, U. (1987). *What the hands reveal about the brain.* Cambridge, MA: MIT Press.

Rymer, R. (1992). A silent childhood. *The New Yorker,* April 20, 43–77.

Sacks, O. (1995). *An anthropologist on Mars.* New York: Alfred A. Knopf.

Spencer, P. E., & Deyo, D. A. (1993). Cognitive and social aspects of deaf children's play. In M. Marschark & M. D. Clark (Eds.), *Psychological perspectives on deafness* (pp. 65–91). Hillsdale, NJ: Lawrence Erlbaum Associates.

Stokoe, W. C. (1960). *Sign Language Structures.* Silver Springs, MD: Linstock Press.

Stokoe, W. C. (1996). The once new field: Sign Language research, or breaking sod in the back forty. *Sign Language Studies, 93,* 379–392.

Tulving, Endel, et al. (1994). Hemispheric encoding/retrieval asymmetry in episodic memory: Positron emission tomography findings. *Proceedings of the National Academy of Sciences*, March 15, 2016–2020.

Vygotsky L. (1962). *Thought and language*. Cambridge, MA: MIT Press.

Vygotsky L. (1978). *Mind in society*. Cambridge, MA: Harvard University Press.

Wilson F. R. (1998). *The hand: How its use shapes the brain, language and human culture*. New York: Pantheon Books.

PART IV
Doing It

Chapter 10

In the School

If you are a teacher and by the time you get to this point in the book decide that you would like to use sign language with your students, how do you begin? Before I go any further with my instructions I would like to stress that there is no set way you must go about this. I have observed many teachers using sign and there have been a great variety of techniques. In the same way that you will find different types of interactions, schedules, curriculum, and classroom arrangements in classrooms across the country, you will find an equally diverse number of teaching approaches for using sign language with hearing students. From the potpourri that follows take what you like and what you believe will work best with your own students and tailor the process to fit these needs in your specific situation.

You may want to use sign with prekindergarten or kindergarten students for classroom management and vocabulary enhancement; or you may be interested in enhancing first or second graders' reading instruction; or you may want to try sign to assist students with their spelling; or you may be interested in using sign to introduce concepts and characters in social studies. Whatever your particular educational goal may be, in all cases your first step will be to learn sign language.

Let me hasten to inform you that you do not have to be a fluent signer. You just need to be a teacher who is willing to learn along with the students. It works best if you can stay a day ahead of them.

This is not always possible, as students will probably be able to re-member the signs more easily than you will, and in the event you forget a sign, they can usually be counted on to supply it. Don't be discouraged by this; they, after all, are usually at the optimal age for learning a language.

There are a number of ways for you to learn sign language. In most communities, there are sign language classes. They can be found in churches, civic groups, schools for the deaf, adult education pro-grams, high schools, community colleges, colleges, and universities. These forms of instruction vary in cost and content, but you should be able to find some sort of class in your area.

Some courses will simply be referred to as sign language classes, and they will generally teach sign language vocabulary in English word order or what is sometimes called *signing exact English* (SEE). In an increasing number of places you will find ASL courses. They are becoming more popular, particularly in higher education, because they meet foreign language requirements. In these classes you will learn the same sign vocabulary, but you will be taught to place the vocabulary in ASL word order. Either type of course will work for your purposes.

If it is not possible to enroll in a sign language class you can learn on your own from books, videotapes, and CD-ROMs. It is a great idea to learn with a colleague or friend. This makes practicing much easier, as you can sign back and forth to each other. Also, if you can locate them where you live, and you usually can, interacting with members of the Deaf community is extremely helpful. I have found that they are generally happy to help you learn and glad to be able to share their language with you.

In any case, no matter what initial route you have taken to acquaint yourself with sign language, you will need to purchase an American Sign Language dictionary. A sign language book may have been as-sociated with the course of instruction you have pursued, but this is usually course-specific with the signs arranged in groups: food, cloth-ing, money, weather, and so on. It is frustrating to locate specific words in such a text.

Arm yourself with an up-to-date dictionary arranged in alphabetical order that provides you with pictures of the signs, describes how to construct them, and explains the history or derivation of the sign. This is critical as ASL is a living language and as such changes and evolves over time. New words become part of the lexicon, and although teaching ASL as a language is not your main purpose, it is important to use correct signs. The history of the ASL sign often gives you a useful memory hook because knowing why the sign is configured in a certain way generally makes it easier to recall it.

A further word about using the correct sign: You will make mistakes. We all do in the normal course of events, when we learn a new language. But do not make up signs. You may be tempted to do this, because of the iconic nature of so many ASL signs. If you were teaching French or Spanish words this would not be an issue. Respect the language and try to use it accurately. In the future, your students may enroll in ASL courses to fulfill their foreign language requirements in high school or college, and learning the proper signs in elementary school will be a wonderful foundation for them.

However, remember that there are individual distinctions in the way signs are formed. If you have more than one sign language teacher you will notice some variations in the way they construct their signs. There are regionalisms in signs, in the same way there are in spoken English. People sign at various rates of speed just as we speak at different paces. People have different-size hands and fingers just as they have different voices and accents. This will make the signs look a bit different, in the same way as it makes the words sound a bit different. All of your friends do not sound exactly the same, and if all your friends signed, they would not sign in exactly the same way.

Understanding that these natural variations in the manner of constructing signs exists should help put you more at ease when you begin to sign with your students. They will all be unique. Also, if you have taken a sign class, you probably noticed that the other students in your class each had their own versions of the signs, much as they have different handwriting. Do try to represent the ASL signs authentically, but do not become tense and rigid and forfeit the beauty of the language itself.

You will need to learn the manual alphabet. This is a one-handed letter-by-letter manual representation of every letter in the English alphabet. Each letter has a specific handshape. It is used to spell English words that have no sign equivalent or to communicate when a person does not know the sign for a word. Using the manual alphabet is referred to as *fingerspelling*. Names of people and places are usually fingerspelled. Within the Deaf community people are given name signs, which frequently combine the first letter of their name with the sign for one of their dominant characteristics. For example, the name sign given to me was the letter *M* (for the first letter of my first name) drawn across the palm of the left hand in the same motion used to sign *nice.*

You need to learn the manual alphabet and become comfortable and fluent with it. Begin by learning the alphabet in sequence. When you have mastered this, fingerspell two- or three-letter words, increasing the length of the word as you gain more manual dexterity. A good way to practice is fingerspelling license plates while driving or recalling the lyrics to songs and fingerspelling them. In a short period your speed and comfort will increase as your fingers become more nimble and sure of themselves. Your ability to read the manual letters will advance if you spend some time practicing in front of a mirror.

After you have mastered the manual alphabet, you want to begin to put together a sign language vocabulary to use with your students. The words you decide to learn will depend on exactly how much sign language you plan to include in your classroom, the age of your students, your educational goals, and ultimately your own level of ease communicating in sign language. Do remember that this is not a race. It is not all-or-nothing. The best way to go about it is gradually and steadily. As you acquire the sign vocabulary, you will also acquire confidence. Far sooner than you think, signing will become second nature to you.

There are several aspects of signing itself that should be considered. You may have covered this in your sign instruction or preparation, but at the risk of being redundant I stress the following: When signing or fingerspelling, signs should be made with the dominant hand. This hand leads the sign, and the other hand is referred to as the *passive hand.* The signs are constructed in the signing space in front of the chest with the arms held in a comfortable manner. Execute the movements slowly and distinctly, maintaining good eye contact with the student or students with whom you are communicating. The students must look at you to understand or read the signs. Strong consistent eye contact by all communicators is important at all times.

I am dividing the remainder of this chapter into several specific areas. The first will be classroom management. In this realm, I believe the ethos in all classrooms could be improved by implementing sign language. The next section will cover early childhood education with a focus on prekindergarten and kindergarten instruction. That section is followed by techniques for using sign to teach reading, spelling, and social studies. All of the procedures I recount are currently being used successfully by teachers in public schools throughout the United States.

CLASSROOM MANAGEMENT

The basic signs you will use to begin will be *yes, no, please, sorry, thank you, hello, good-bye*. The students will learn the signs faster and pay closer attention to you if you do not voice for these kinds of exchanges. This reliance on eye contact is a primary reason sign is so effective for classroom management. You may have to say and sign the directions the first few times until the pupils are sure of the meaning, but once that has been established, use only the sign. Gradually add more signs as the days go on. *Walk, slow (down), sit (down), stop, now, wait, noisy, quiet, start, line up, help, come, go, outside, inside, toilet, wash, drink, eat, hungry, and thirsty* are all appropriate signs with which to continue.

Listen to yourself and add the signs for the words that you use as you give directions. The sign vocabulary you acquire for classroom management will be the same English vocabulary you currently use. One of the advantages of switching to a signing modality is that you encourage the students to attend to you without constantly reminding them to do so. The classroom becomes quieter. It is a more pleasant place. There is an *absence* of nagging, or reminders to pay attention, or look at me, or eyes front. You do not hear exasperation or animus in the paralanguage that often accompanies a teacher's spoken directions at times when fatigue or frustration begins to take over.

The next group of words you would try to teach are the feeling words. Almost all of these words are iconic and are easy for the students to learn. Students are better able to understand and relate to their own feelings after you have explored them together in class and they have learned to express these feelings by using the appropriate signs. Teach them the signs for words like *proud, mad, sad, sick, happy, tired, sleepy, hungry,* and *thirsty*. During this teaching time, it is also a good idea to include some of the actions they may engage in when they have these feelings, such as *hit, shove,* or *push,* and *take*. As the children in the Walker School (Chapter 7) learned, it is fine to have and acknowledge these feelings, but you must not act on them in hurtful ways.

Go slowly with the signs. Do not try to introduce more than the students can learn. Try to use them consistently. Encourage the class to sign to each other and to you. Some of the children will readily take to this; others will be more reticent about independently signing. If your class is like most typical groups you will find that some of your less able students will be very good at signing and really shine.

The students will usually ask you how to sign words. You often will not know how to sign them. When this occurs, it is a good idea to have a signing dictionary in the classroom for you and the students to consult. If you do not know a sign, you can look it up. The children can, too. Engaging in such research with the children is a positive exercise. It specifically teaches dictionary skills and in a general sense demonstrates the way answers can be found in books. Everyone gains from this experience.

Even the youngest children in kindergarten classes are eager to discover how to construct the signs. When the sign dictionary is left out in the classroom on a table or shelf, easily accessible to them, students will often consult it on their own initiative. By providing young learners with this opportunity, you not only expose them to dictionary skills but show that teachers do not have all the answers. Teachers locate answers in books, and if they model themselves after their teacher, they themselves can find answers if they are willing to expend the energy to do so. Establishing this pattern during their formative years should stand students in good stead when they meet future educational challenges.

When do you mention what you are doing? This will vary, depending on your own point of view and the age of your students. I have seen prekindergarten classes in which the teacher offers no initial explanation for the signing component. The children take naturally to the sign and undoubtedly believe it is a usual or normal way for their teacher to behave. They have no previous experience of school, so as far as they know, all teachers teach this way. For them signing is just a routine part of school.

As the school year progresses, teachers who have made no initial reference to the signing in class generally mention that sign is the language of the Deaf community and offer some further background about sign and the condition of deafness in keeping with the age and interest of the students. In regions of the country where there are a significant number of individuals who are deaf and use ASL, teachers will often invite Deaf children or adults to visit the class and interact with the students.

When teachers introduce sign to students in higher grades who have had no previous signing experience in public school classes, they are forced to offer some explanation for the new mode of communication they are using. They tend to keep it simple, explaining that sign language is used by the Deaf community and that they are learning it in school for a number of reasons: Namely, it will make their classrooms quieter, they will soon be able to communicate with people who are Deaf, and they will be able to communicate with each other without talking. Some teachers mention signs' educational advantages, but this is often not a strong student motivator.

In most instances the teacher or the school itself sends a notice home informing the parents about the signing that will be taking place in the classroom. In addition to this information, some teachers will send home weekly newsletters describing the signs they will be teaching in class and asking the parents to help the students learn the signs. A number of teachers have sent home videotapes they have created of the signs they are using. Sometimes these tapes feature the students.

This is a good idea, because it is an opportunity to communicate with the primary care givers and opens up a neutral channel for interaction between the home and the school. I mention the neutral aspect of sign because some teachers have students whose parents cannot read English. It is difficult to involve such parents in the child's education. Even if they would like to participate, they often feel self-conscious and inadequate. Sign language presents a chance to break through such barriers with some parents. After all, no one is expected to know sign language, so it really levels the playing field.

How much interaction you decide to initiate between the home and school will be dependent on the situation in which you find yourself. Often it becomes an exciting, worthwhile exchange; in other instances, it can become frustrating, particularly if material you have spent time creating shows up unread and unused. In any case, the students will learn from the sign experience they receive in the classroom and are not dependent on involvement at home. No matter what has happened to sign material designed for use at home, the signing will undoubtedly find its way home, as almost all children are excited about learning it and tend to share it with others because they enjoy knowing something that they know better than their siblings or parents.

PREKINDERGARTEN AND KINDERGARTEN

In prekindergarten and kindergarten you will be implementing sign language for classroom management, as indicated in the previous section. Begin on the first day of class. The children will accept it as a natural part of school and in the majority of cases understand and respond to the classroom management signs by the end of the first week of school. Most classrooms for these grades are divided into various activity centers. Teach the children sign names for the centers in their room during the first or second week of class.

During the opening circle time include signs for the key concepts you introduce each day. These are generally words that refer to weather, seasons, holidays, activities, and attendance. Sign the word and say the word. Ask the students to sign and say the word. Some will be better able to form their hands into the signs than others. You can help them by moving their hands into the correct shapes. Also, let them help each other. This assisting phenomenon usually occurs without any prompting.

Include signing with your reading and storytelling. Teach the signs for several key words from a story before you read the story. When you read these words in the story, ask the children to make the signs. For instance, if you were telling the story of Goldilocks and the Three Bears, you could teach the signs for *bear, chair*, and *bed*. Each time you reach one of the words as you read the story, wait for the children to make the appropriate sign for the word.

In each story it is up to you to select the key words. The particular words, as well as the number of words, will depend on your group's ability and your teaching objectives. Sometimes you may want to describe the meaning of the word as you teach the children the sign. The iconic nature of many signs often helps students understand word meanings. It is far easier for students to remember words when their meaning has been clarified.

Check whether the students can define the words and have understood the story by asking simple questions about the words or story that can be answered yes or no. Have them sign their yes or no answers. When you look at their hands, you will quickly ascertain who needs more assistance and who knows the answers. Signing of answers provides an easy, efficient way to assess comprehension.

When you introduce the letters of the alphabet or review them, teach the manual sign for each of the letters. It is a fine idea also to teach a sign word for each of the letters. You can decide the words. They can all be animals, or they can be words from the vocabulary lists for their first reading books, or you could select a variety of words that do not have a concrete object to picture. These would be words like *run, fast, take*.

When the children know the entire alphabet, they should be able to begin to fingerspell. Start with two- and three-letter words. Students will soon be able to fingerspell their own names. They really enjoy doing this, and it can add a new dimension to circle time. In a like manner, teach the students the signs for the numbers and colors when they appear in your curriculum. If this means you are attempting to cover too many new signs at one time, you may have to make some minor adjustments in your teaching plans.

A good way to get more practice time with signs is to incorporate them into the usual songs, poems, and games you would use with kindergarten children. "Old Mac Donald" sung by using signs for each of the animals is a favorite. Fingerspelling the "Alphabet Song" as they sing makes it much more fun. Signing key words in nursery rhymes such as *little, lamb*, and *school* adds to the enjoyment, as well as the educational benefit. Alphabet bingo played with signs is an example of a game easily enhanced with signs. In the sign version, the teacher signs the letter with no voicing and the students sign and say the letter as they cover the appropriate letter on an alphabet bingo card. There are commercially available cards that have about eight upper- and lowercase letters on each card or you can make your own.

Another game children really love is a counting game in which they sign the number one, and then an object such as one banana, two apples, three oranges, and so on. They can add colors as they learn them, such as *one yellow banana*, and additional adjectives such as *large*, creating *one large yellow banana, two little red apples*, and so forth. The counting nouns can be foods or animals or categories such as families, using *mother, father, daughter, son*, or they can be independent unassociated words that simply represent sign vocabulary from your normal curriculum. The counting game provides practice with the signs and the manual numbers, as well as introducing noun phrases and mathematical concepts.

You should interject the signs at your own pace. Do not put pressure on yourself. Rather stay within the bounds of your own comfort zone. Use your usual curriculum, simply enriching it with the sign language. The four- and five-year-old children whom you will be teaching will take to sign as ducks take to water. They will be happily, actively involved in learning. For your part you will likely love it. I have never known an early childhood teacher who did not continue to use sign language with a class once they had started. Teachers see the benefit of sign and refuse to give it up.

READING

In kindergarten classes in which sign has been part of the traditional curriculum since the first day of school, using sign for reading instruction is an easy transition for both the teacher and the students, though previous experience with sign is not necessary. It can be combined with any method of reading instruction or curriculum you currently use. Sometimes when you first begin to use signs to teach reading, it may seem strange and appear to be an extra layer. However, you should soon be able to recognize its benefit.

Teach the children the manual alphabet as you determine their ability to recognize letters. This can be incorporated in your usual sequence, either in alphabetical order or in specific letter groups. When the students have mastered the alphabet and the manual letters, many teachers introduce the short vowel sounds and all the consonant sounds with illustrative sign sentences such as *a* says "ah," as in *apple*.

Connecting the letter with a word picture illustrative of its sound will later provoke students' memory when they begin to learn to read. Teachers who use this technique report that when students are having difficulty sounding out a word, they merely form the manual letter and hold up their hand. Seeing the manual letter sparks a response that enables them to recall the sound from the sentence they learned earlier. This is a far more effective method for search and recall than providing an oral prompt. (See Chapter 6 for a detailed explanation of brain activity that illustrates why this is true.)

With beginning readers, ESL students, or children who have had difficulty with traditional reading methods, start by including a physical object that represents the word you are teaching. This concrete object will be eliminated later. For instance, you could begin by teaching *bat, hat, cat, I, touch, the*. Show the children an object such as a hat, say and sign *hat*, and display a card on which the word *hat* is written. Have the children read the word *hat* aloud and sign the word *hat*. Repeat this until you feel the students can read and sign *hat* and know that the word refers to the hat they see.

Work with small groups of children. Teach three or four words at one time. If three or four words are too many or too few words for your students to learn easily, adjust the number of words. Each day review the previous day's words before you begin to learn new ones. Your goal is to maintain their interest and pleasure in the process, not to frustrate them.

Every day they see, hear, say, and sign the words with accompanying concrete objects or pictures to establish the meaning of the word. Very shortly they have learned enough words to begin to form sentences. With just the six words I have suggested, they can sign and read three different sentences. You can place the word cards on a chalk rail in a sentence sequence and ask them to read the sentences, signing and saying each word.

You can laminate the word cards so that you will be able to reuse them. You and the students can construct books featuring the simple sentences and stories you create together. If you currently have books of a similar nature, as you undoubtedly do, make word cards for the vocabulary in the books and assemble objects that illustrate their meaning and proceed as I have indicated in my example.

Begin with word families as I have suggested or select words with very different visual configurations. There are two schools of thought on this. Some educators believe it is far easier for children to learn to read and recognize words that do not resemble other words and suggest this is the better way to begin to teach them to read. In my example, *cat, hat*, and *bat* look similar. If you would like to go the other route, you would begin with three words such as *mouse, car*, and *telephone*.

No matter what procedure you decide to follow, work with the reading materials that are available to you, within the framework of your school's educational objectives. Maintain a controlled vocabulary at first to enhance the potential for student success. As their reading signing vocabulary increases, cycle back to the words your students learned during the first few days of instruction, consistently reviewing. Phonics can be incorporated easily as blends and digraphs are added, so that children can begin to recognize new words by using elements that are already familiar to them.

Continue to include the concrete physical objects until you are certain your students understand that the words they are signing and saying represent these objects. When you feel confident they fully comprehend this, you can eliminate the physical objects. This may occur within the first month; with some students it will take longer. You may be using objects with some groups after you have eliminated them with other groups. Think of the objects as training wheels.

You retain the signing as an integral part of the reading method. The signs become particularly useful as they represent verbs and articles for which we have no object or picture. The signs themselves become the picture or pattern for the word. This helps children remember words such as *the, that, and, fast,* and *after.* The new sign vocabulary for any story or book is introduced before you begin to read. During this time meanings are explored and are explained if necessary. The iconic nature of many signs or the description of their derivation often makes their meaning transparent. This helps the emergent reader with comprehension.

Signing games can play a significant role in learning sight words, letter-sound associations, and concept development. A game you can use for sight word practice is tic-tac-toe. In this adaptation, the students work in groups of four. Each group has a blank tic-tac-toe board and two different-colored packs of word cards, for example, yellow and green. The yellow two-person team begins by turning over the first yellow card. A sight word is printed on the card. One yellow student team member silently reads the word, then signs the word, and then says the word aloud. If this is correctly done, the team selects the box on the board where they would like to place the yellow card. Now it is time for the green team to turn over a green card. The pupil silently reads, signs, and says the word correctly, then the green team places the green card on the board. The yellow team selects its second card and the second member of the yellow team takes a turn reading, signing and saying the word. If it is correct the team selects its second box on the tic-tac-toe board and the play moves to the green team's second player. The turn is forfeited if there are any mistakes. Mistakes are identified by the opposing team. The teacher moves around observing the groups and acting as final arbitrator of signs. Each game proceeds until there is a green or yellow winner.

A game that helps children form letter-sound associations is played with a stack of sight word cards with two different initial consonant blends, for instance, *br* and *sh.* The words can be *bring, break, bright, broom*, and *sheep, ship, shoe,* and *show*. The children can do this in two teams. The first word card is removed from the stack and displayed. It may be *bring*. The student silently reads the card, signs the word, and then says the word aloud, while placing the word card in the location designated for words beginning with *br*. This can be a card pocket, a magnet board, or a chalk rail. The next card is displayed and the first student from the other team silently reads the card, signs the word, and then says the word while placing it in the appropriate spot for either a *br* or a *sh* word. If there are any mistakes, the other members of the team can help the student. It is a group effort. When all eight words are in their respective spots, each team gets a chance to read, sign, and say the entire list of words in unison for the other team.

Finally, a game that helps children's concept development can be played by using a variety of objects. When you first start to play the game only use objects from two distinct groups of words such as *clothes* and *kitchen*. Before you begin the game, print the names of all the objects on the board or on a flip chart and designate a kitchen and clothes closet area in the room. Place the objects in the center of the circle and have the children take turns. In this instance the objects can be *shoe, shirt, coat, hat,* and *bowl, spoon, plate,* and *cup*. They select an object from the pile, sign the object's name, and point to the appropriate written word as they pronounce it, and complete their turn by placing the object in the correct predesignated area, in this instance, either clothes closet or kitchen.

Any of these three suggested signing games can be adapted to fit your own students' learning needs. They can be made easier or more difficult. For instance, the tic-tac-toe game can be played with very few simple words with more repetition. The object game can be played with three or four different groups of objects, making the classification task more difficult. Any of the games can be played with individuals or teams or entire classes or individual groups within a single class. You will get optimal results if you consistently strive to mix at least one good signer with one good reader.

READING WITH OLDER CHILDREN

Sign is helpful for older children in higher grades as well. When sign is used with older students in the regular classroom you have children of varying abilities, from above- to below-average. Often children who were unable to learn how to read through the modalities previously presented to them will be able to read with the addition of signing. Their recall becomes better and they are able to retain and remember the words. The students who have the most difficulty with reading are the ones sign appears to help the most.

When using sign with older students, you follow the same general procedure indicated for beginning readers with a few variations. You do not include the physical object, because it is assumed that by this time students understand that words stand for or represent things. You will usually start with the sight words. Traditionally students are taught to focus either on the configuration of the word or on the sounds contained within the word.

With the signing method you select the word you want to teach. Introduce the word visually in print, then sign and say the word. For the students it is executing the sign, hearing the word, and seeing the word. Always have the students sign with you. Explain the rationale behind the signs or the iconic nature of the sign to establish meanings for each sight word. In sign language there are different signs to express different meanings. For instance, the sign for *like*, meaning "affection," is different than the sign for *like*, meaning "same." This aspect provides a wonderful opportunity to further students' comprehension of words.

Usually sign is introduced to a small group of your lowest readers first. The other children in the class, your average and high readers, who are often busy doing seat work at the time, are generally intrigued by what is happening in your small group and will soon begin to pick up the signs on their own, learn them from their classmates, and pester you to include them in the signing group. It is up to you to decide what to do. Many teachers will have the slow readers, who now know the signs, teach them to the stronger readers. This approach tends to help build student confidence, and children develop a high regard for themselves and their schoolwork.

A fine example of this kind of shared learning occurred in a first-grade class where I observed a lesson. The teacher uses sign with her class regularly and they are quite good signers. On the day I was there, she began by reviewing a story poem the children all knew. It was displayed on a word-picture chart on an easel. The children all said and signed the poem line by line together, without any mistakes. Next, the teacher said she would teach them three new words for their new story poem.

She taught them *travel, visit,* and *together.* The sign and the written word were introduced for each of the three words. The children practiced the signs with each other. Some helped their classmates place their fingers correctly. For example, the sign for *friend* is made with the index fingers of both hands; a few of the children tried to make the sign with the pinkie fingers, and they were corrected by their classmates.

The new story poem was displayed on the easel, and a child was selected to indicate the words with a pointer throughout the lesson. The teacher said and signed the title. The students repeated the title, saying and signing it together. The teacher made corrections quietly. All repeated the title, signing and saying it together. The procedure was followed with each line. When the first stanza was completed, the first stanza was repeated, using sign only. The entire procedure was repeated with the second stanza. Then, the complete poem was read and signed together. After the entire poem was read and signed, it was repeated without voicing, using sign only.

A Visit with a Whale

> I will travel to the sea
> and visit with a whale.
> Together we will laugh and play
> with me upon his tail.
>
> I will learn about the sea
> and when the day is through.
> He will say good-bye my friend
> when may I visit you?

Next, the children were divided into groups of four and placed at small tables. The groups had been formed by the teacher, and each group contained a good reader and a good signer. The children worked together to complete their assignment. When I observed their progress I could see that the good signers were not usually the best readers, and vice versa. It was a clear sharing of strengths to accomplish their task.

Each group was given the poem cut into nine strips of phrases in a mixed-up order. The first child signed the first phrase to the other three children in the group. The children did this in an established pattern in a clockwise rotation. All tried to read the signs being presented by the student. When they figured it out, they placed the phrase in its proper place on a plain sheet of paper. They glued the strip down only when they were sure it was in the correct spot. The next child signed another phrase, and the children decided where it should be placed. They constantly checked each other and corrected each other's handshapes and spoken English words.

The groups all completed their poems at about the same time. When they were done, they handed their work to the teacher. If she agreed that the poem was in the right order, she complimented them, and they went to their spot on the rug and quietly signed to each other, laughed a bit, and talked quietly.

When all the groups had completed their assigned task, the teacher rejoined the entire class on the rug. During the exercise she was moving about the room among the groups, offering help and encouragement where needed. Now, the entire class signed and read the poem together. This time there were no mistakes. All of the children remained very involved throughout the lesson. It was one of the best examples I have ever seen of groups of children learning together in a healthy classroom climate.

The preceding scenario demonstrates how sign language and the activities that accompany it are used to teach reading. Children enjoy working together with the signs and words. In this instance the teacher created her own material. Her example could be followed with other poems, nursery rhymes, or song lyrics that form a portion of your current curriculum. Also, teachers can either make or purchase flash cards with signs or letters from the manual alphabet and printed words on them. These cards can be used by pairs or small groups of children to practice their signs and words.

There are manual alphabet fonts for the typewriter or computer, so additional teaching materials can be created easily. Individual seat work sheets are made with the sign for the word and the icon shapes for the letters of the manual alphabet. The student has to print or write the word in English. This helps with spelling, word recognition, and penmanship.

An interesting phenomenon that must occur over and over again because it was reported by so many teachers is the intriguing ability children have to remember the English word itself after it has been signed. What the teachers recount is that while children are reading, they can recall the sign for the word before they can recall the word itself. The sign actually gives the students the word. By either seeing the sign or making the sign they are able to recall and say the word.

Sometimes when students run into difficulty with a word while they are reading aloud, teachers prompt them by making the sign for the word. At other times, teachers have observed that students who are having trouble articulating a word make the sign for the word themselves, then pronounce the word. This happens spontaneously with no prompting from the teacher.

Any of the games described at the end of the previous section can be used with older children as well. In addition there are other games that students like to play that reinforce their ability to read, to sign, and to comprehend. Three such games are On the Road, Sign the Answer, and Translation Trouble.

On the Road is played in a circle with the teacher starting the story by saying, "I went on this road and I saw a _____." The first student fills in the blank by signing a word without voicing. The next student says the word the previous student has signed. The third student in the circle fingerspells the word. The game can either continue with the fourth person seeing and signing additional items, such as a tree and a house, or by starting at the beginning again with just one item. The way you use this game will depend on the ability of your students, as well as your educational goals.

Sign the Answer is a game that can be used to review vocabulary and practice spelling. You make up a series of questions that can be answered with words from your specific teaching material. The sentences might be "What do you wear on your foot?" or "What do you put mustard on?" The teacher asks the questions and the students sign the answers. You can also have them fingerspell the answer after they have signed it. This game is played by teams or by individual players.

Translation Trouble can be played with a small circle of students; however, it is most often played with dyads. Once they have become fairly accomplished signers, it is a great way for students to practice together. Student A makes a sign and Student B says and fingerspells the word. Then the action is reversed. You can also have a third person who watches the signing and spelling dyad and serves as a referee. When it is played in a group, the play proceeds around the circle.

SPELLING

In the previous sections on reading I have mentioned fingerspelling in association with reading. It is a natural way to incorporate the manual alphabet and enhance the students' spelling ability and will usually form a regular portion of the instruction when you are using sign in the classroom. In this segment I would like to remind you of the singular benefit that fingerspelling and the manual alphabet can provide for students even when it constitutes the only sign enhancement in the curriculum.

There are a vast number of instances in which children's ability to spell has been measurably enhanced by merely using the manual alphabet to fingerspell spelling words. To achieve this you simply teach the manual alphabet and tell the students to fingerspell as they orally say the letters in a word. They can silently practice fingerspelling words to each other in pairs. Sometimes you may want to use a third child as an observer to catch any errors.

A worthwhile adaptation to incorporate with the fingerspelling-the-word technique is to have the children cover the fingerspelled letter, if it is silent in the word. They do this by fingerspelling the word with their dominant hand, as they normally would. When they reach a letter that is silent in the word, they cover the fingerspelled letter with their other hand, by placing the open flat hand, palm facing their body, in front of the silent letter. A student who is spelling *cake* fingerspells c-a-k-e with their right hand. Immediately after the student fingerspells *e*, they would place their left hand in front of the final *e*.

This technique is useful for identifying the silent letters in words. Students know that the letter is there because they have formed it with their fingers and signaled its silent property with their other hand. This procedure offers a powerful memory stimulus for their spelling and fosters children's ability to pronounce words. Make sure the fingerspelling operation is firmly established before you add this variation to the process.

An entire group's spelling list can quickly be evaluated by having the students fingerspell the words without voicing. The teacher pronounces the spelling word, and the students silently fingerspell the word. As the teacher observes all of the students it is easy to spot the students who are incorrectly spelling the word. The spelling correction can be made immediately, and the students do not continue to retain the incorrect spelling in their mind. This activity is very useful, because each time a student writes the word incorrectly it reinforces the mistake and embeds it more deeply. There is not enough time for a teacher to listen to all the children orally spell their spelling words. By implementing these techniques, you should see a dramatic improvement in students' memory as evidenced by their ability to recall spelling words.

If you would like to test this phenomenon yourself, do the following: After you have mastered the manual alphabet, fingerspell the items you would like to purchase before you go to the grocery store. This creates a kinesthetic list that is difficult to lose. If you are like most people, the fingerspelling will be a marvelous memory aid and you will not forget any items. Do not make the shopping list too long, at least on the first trial. You can also experiment with this technique in another context by fingerspelling any interesting names, book titles, or phone numbers you hear on your car radio that you would like to recall when you get home.

SOCIAL STUDIES AND OTHER CONTENT AREAS

Subject areas other than reading or spelling can be enhanced with sign language. It is routinely used in many schools from first grade through fifth grade for social studies, history, music, drama, science, geography, and even math. In these settings it clearly supports content by defining concepts and aiding memory.

I observed a fourth-grade social studies class that was studying the history of the state of Maryland. The teacher always augments her lessons with sign language, so the children have a respectable sign language vocabulary to draw upon. During the day I was there, she would remind them of a sign they knew and they would join her in forming the sign. In other instances the students would produce the sign before they were prompted.

The focus of the lesson was the governor of Maryland and the first Lord Baltimore. This history centered around the Calvert family. It was easy to describe the relationships of George, Cecil, and Leonard with signs. The students knew these relationship signs and freely used them. They already knew the signs for *king* and *queen*, which also figured in the tale. Names such as *Henrietta, Maria*, and *Charles* were fingerspelled.

A phrase occurred in the lesson that was not understood; the students did not know what the term *indentured servant* meant. The teacher led them to the meaning by taking them from a known sign to an unknown sign. First, she asked them to make the sign for *work*. They all knew this sign and formed it by tapping the wrist of the right *S* hand on the back of the wrist of the left *S* hand with a double movement. Then she taught them the sign for *indentured servant*, which is formed with the wrists of both *s* hands crossed in front of the body, palms facing down; then the arms are moved in a large flat circle in front of the body with a double movement. This sign graphically demonstrated the meaning of the word. The teacher pointed this out to the students by explaining how this sign showed that you could not get away from the work; Your arms were locked in this crossed position and just went around in a circular motion.

The students in this class remained very interested and involved in the material throughout the lesson I observed. The teacher reported that this was the usual level of participation. She stressed that augmenting her instruction with sign language has had several benefits. In her opinion, it sparks student interest, performance, comprehension, and retention. She believes that sign is the reason her students achieve higher grades on standard achievement tests than comparable fourth-grade students in other classes. Before she used sign, her students did not earn elevated scores on standard measures.

Teachers in other subject areas can use sign to enhance their programs in a manner similar to that used by the social studies teacher. However, to be effective, sign does not even have to constitute as much of the lesson as it did in the social studies lesson. For example, when students respond to a teacher's questions concerning content, in any subject area, by signing yes or no without voicing, response variations can be seen easily. By quietly observing the inconsistencies a teacher can make a quick assessment of individual students' comprehension and make the necessary corrections.

Children's receptive and expressive skills can be demonstrated by having them indicate whether events in a narrative are fact or fantasy by signing these words. They can respond with feeling signs such as *sad, happy, nice, mean, afraid,* and *brave* to illustrate their understanding of a historical, contemporary, or fictional character's emotional response. By signing *yes, no, never, always, some,* or *all* in response to verbal queries about any subject, they will exhibit their grasp of the content.

CONCLUSION

This chapter has covered many classroom settings. I have recounted the use of sign for classroom management, early childhood education, social studies and other content areas; its specific use for emergent and established readers; as well as the use of the manual alphabet and fingerspelling as a fine support for spelling.

I have tried to describe clearly the techniques used by the various teachers I have observed, and the teachers who have worked with me on research projects. You will note that the teachers have gone about incorporating sign language in the classroom in slightly different ways. To be sure, there are similarities, but they have all adapted the signing component to their own aptitudes and their individual students' needs. The three attributes they each possess are an interest in improving their ability to teach children, a belief that sign language offers educational benefits, and a willingness to try. With these three qualities, the teachers have begun dancing with words.

Chapter II

In the Home

There will be both short- and long-term rewards for using sign language with babies and young children in the home. The short-term advantages will center around facilitating communication with your child, and the long-term advantages will center around enhancing your child's ability to communicate with others. The long-term advantages may not even figure into your desire to use sign language with your child; however, they may come into play sooner than you would think.

In today's world the use of sign language within the general population is proliferating. It is respected as a legitimate language and as such is taught and accepted in academic settings from grade school through university. Sign language interpreters are regularly seen at public meetings, church services, and political events. It has become routine to see sign language on television, whether in commercials, as the focus of dramas, or in the small round circles at the bottom of the screen that often accompany religious programming. Throughout the variety of television offerings there are abundant examples of signing from "Sesame Street" to "Pennsylvania Avenue."

Currently there are also significant changes in the way Deaf children are being educated and will be educated in the future that increase the likelihood a hearing child will encounter a Deaf child in the public school classroom. To meet new legislative requirements initiated by the Americans with Disabilities Act, many Deaf children, who would have previously received their education in a homogeneous setting in a school specifically designed for educating Deaf children, are now being mainstreamed into public schools, receiving their education in an inclusive setting.

Five years from now, when a child born today enters kindergarten, they will almost certainly find a Deaf child in the school. It will be a boon to both children if communication can occur easily between them. A child who has been introduced to sign language in the home and has learned it concurrently with English to facilitate communication with the parents will be in a wonderful position to communicate with such a schoolmate.

The long-term rewards for the child do not stop with communication opportunities in primary school. The many educational benefits for children's literacy, detailed in this book, await. Plus, the ASL head start they possess can aid their acquisition of ASL as a foreign language, if they select it in high school or college. Even in the rare circumstance in which they do not have an opportunity to use sign during the intervening years between childhood and second-language learning, they should still be able to recall the basic ASL vocabulary they learned in the home. In the same way that nursery rhymes can be recalled in later years, sign language is firmly embedded and remains with the child throughout life, ready to be used.

Although these long-term positive attributes associated with sign language learning exist, when you decide to try sign language with your infant or young child, it will usually be because of the short-term advantages it offers. You want to be able to communicate with your child more easily. Specifically, you want to understand your child's needs. Is the child hungry? Does something hurt? Would the child like to go for a walk? Using sign language can help clarify the child's demands and offers a smooth transition on the communication road from babyhood to childhood. Through nonverbal dialogue with your child you can achieve a satisfying base for their verbal communication. Knowing sign language will enhance the child's ability to comprehend meaning in both the expressive and receptive modes, and it will actually support the use of verbal English.

How and when do you begin? In this chapter I am relying on the experience of mothers and fathers who have used sign language with their babies. In some instances, they began using sign to fix something; and in others, they began using it to enhance something. Some families had babies who would fit the newly coined term *high-maintenance*. These babies were fussy and cried a lot, making it difficult to understand what they wanted. Other families had babies who were bright and inquisitive and appeared eager to communicate. These babies were attempting to enter into a dialogue with their parents, although they had no language to use as currency.

If the parents are trying to fix something, they generally begin by introducing signs for words that are specific to their concerns about the child's physical needs. For instance, they might begin by teaching the signs for *drink, food, hungry, tired, down, up, in,* and *out.* Do not overload the child at first—or ever, for that matter. Slow and consistent progress is best.

Select the signs you feel would help to foster a better understanding of the child's needs. Even fairly young babies know what they want, but they have no way to express their desires, other than to cry and carry on. When they are presented with a means to communicate, they will use it. Well before the onset of verbal language, babies are able to communicate in the manual language of sign. Make the sign distinctly, associate it with an action or object, and pronounce its English referent clearly. Be certain you have the baby's attention and the baby can see your hand as it forms the sign. You may need to adapt the signing space to a smaller box. After you construct the sign a few times, mold the baby's hand into the shape of the sign with your own hand.

A simple sign to begin with is *up.* This is made with the extended index finger pointing up, the palm is facing forward, and the hand moved upward a short distance. Repeat this every time you pick up the baby, molding the baby's hand into the correct configuration. Soon the baby will sign the word for you. You begin to add signs when you are sure the first sign has been established.

Parents of the bright and bouncy children begin in much the same way. They can usually proceed at a faster pace because they are not concerned with other needs. Their initial signs are often the same words that the high-maintenance babies learn. These signs relate to the child's daily care and represent words that are typically used with the child.

The parent or care giver working with the baby will need to learn the signs and the manual alphabet. As in the case of teachers, a parent can take sign classes, view videos, or use computers. You will also need a comprehensive up-to-date ASL dictionary, containing pictures of the signs and descriptions detailing how they are formed. In addition, as the child gets older you will undoubtedly want to purchase some flash cards and games. There are also some children's books using sign, which may appeal to you.

What about making up signs, in essence creating your own gestures to use with your child? Will this work? Yes, to a certain extent it would; you and your child would have a secret code that you could use to facilitate your communication with each other. But that is where it would start and end. No one else would know what the gestures meant. So the answer is no. Do not make up a whole new system. It may work for you and your child, but it is limiting and does not present the full advantage of introducing authentic vocabulary from an authentic language.

It may require a bit more effort to learn and teach the real ASL signs, but it is well worth it. What would be the sense of making up nonsense words if you were trying to teach a child a language? You could call a ball a *ron*, you could call a spoon a *det*, or you could call a bed a *ait*. Now the parent and the child would know that *ron* meant "ball," that *det* meant "spoon," and that *ait* meant "bed." But no one else would, and that is exactly the point. Making up gestures would be comparable to this.

When your child goes to nursery school there is a good chance that the child will encounter teachers, aides, and other students who know and use some ASL sign vocabulary. When your child watches television authentic signs are seen during commercials and regular programming, in addition to its use as interpretation of content. Stick with the ASL vocabulary when you communicate with your child. The legitimate language offers far greater immediate and long-range benefits.

After all, it is estimated that 15 million people in the United States, including members of both the Deaf and hearing communities communicate in ASL. At any given time there are over one hundred thousand people learning ASL, both in formal institutions of learning and in classes conducted by social agencies, churches, and other groups and it is estimated that thirteen million people can communicate in sign language. Why not have your child join the other students?

In an attempt to offer a realistic picture of what transpires in the home I offer some facts about a little boy called Donavon. He was what his mother refers to as a fussy child. When he was nine months of age, he could not talk, but he was very whiny. His mother wanted to have a more peaceful environment. She was searching for a way to allow him to communicate. She hit upon the idea of using sign language with him. She acquired a sign language dictionary and learned the signs for basic expressions she thought he needed to know and taught him the signs.

She began with signs that centered around the dinner table. He learned how to sign and respond to *please, eat, drink*. His signing food vocabulary quickly expanded to include *apple, pasta*, and *cookie*. Soon he could combine his signs and sign *eat please*.

When he was a year old, he learned the sign for *bath*. He would delight in signing *bath* and running down the hall to the bathroom for his bath. His mother showed him the sign for *out*. After that, he would sign *out* to indicate his desire to go outside and play. He would ask for help by signing *help*. And he would sign *again* whenever he wanted something repeated. When he wanted more, generally an item of food, he would sign *more*.

By the time he was fourteen months old, he knew and used more ASL signs than spoken English words. However, he was beginning to speak, but would usually only use one modality for a word, rarely signing and saying a word at the same time. His mother described him as being happier and calmer and as exhibiting a proud attitude and a satisfied expression at being able to "talk" with signs.

She used sign to teach him colors. When he was about two she hung a wall chart of the manual alphabet in his room at his eye level. Unbeknownst to him, she watched him teach himself the manual alphabet. Later he would sign "The Alphabet Song" and sign his interpretation of the letters.

On his own initiative he taught the signs to the other little children at his church nursery school. Before very long all the children in the class were signing together. Some of the children would say the word when they signed it. Others would just sign it. In the nursery school the children would always sign the word if they knew the sign. Donavon continued to use only one language for most words.

His mother observed that his ability to sign served to boost his self-esteem and to provoke positive feedback from the general public. When he was in the bank or at the bakery and he received a free lollipop or cookie he would sign *thank you*. The tellers and clerks thought this was clever and responded with smiles and positive comments.

When I last communicated with Donavon's mother, he was two

years, four months old. He can now talk very well and people tell her he is quite articulate for his age. At the moment, she mainly uses sign to help Donavon memorize Bible verses. She shows him the signs for the key words. It is working wonderfully and he remembers his verses better than she does.

Donavon knows and recognizes the digits 0 through 9 and does not confuse 6 and 9. He can count from 1 to 100 with the aid of a counting chart. She heard him do this on his own one morning while he was waiting for her to get him up. He also can identify most letters, only confusing *d*, *b*, *p*, and *g*. He knows the sounds of the letters as well and attempts to sound out words. He is good at this, particularly when there is a picture of the word.

Donavon has a new baby sister. He signs to her, and although she is just six weeks old, he tries to shape her hands and arms into signs to sign back to him. He manipulates her tiny fingers and hands and fashions conversations with his sister. He loves doing this (V. Whalen, personal communication, July 25, 1999).

Donavon's experience with sign language is typical of what occurs in the home when parents present sign to a child as an alternate language. Including sign language in the communication mix can eliminate the frustration both parent and child often experience as they attempt to comprehend each other. It fosters pleasant discourse, clarifies meaning, and creates better understanding between them. With the keener understanding, there also comes an authentic grasp of content.

Sign does not hinder language development in any way; rather, it fosters it. It picks up on the natural visual acuity young children possess and uses it to the child's advantage. The point that Donavon is advanced in his number recognition, and actually taught himself the manual alphabet, attests to this fact.

The manual alphabet is an important tool for children to learn, offering a number of physical as well as educational advantages. It helps generate the fine motor coordination that children will need when they begin to write and print letters. An established developmental link exists between handwriting and the cognitive skills necessary for reading. However, well before children are able to form letters with a pencil, they can form letters with the manual alphabet. Using the manual alphabet will activate the same formative link to reading as printing, but it may have an even greater effect on children's literacy because it can occur far earlier in their maturation process.

There are many types of alphabet books with pictures of the manual alphabet for children. You can use several. Also, there are colorful alphabet wall charts like the one Donavon's mother used, as well as manual alphabet wallpaper strips or borders. Be certain that whatever you use can be easily viewed by the child. It must be large enough, clearly drawn, and located or shown to the child at their eye level.

Teach the child the manual alphabet in the same day-to-day way you normally teach the written alphabet. Construct the manual letter whenever you indicate the printed letter. Form the manual letter when you emphasize a letter sound. When you read any alphabet book or encounter single letters displayed on a page or on a sign, construct the manual letter and ask the child to do the same thing. Encourage the child to model after you, making the manual letter whenever you do. You can assist by forming the child's hand into the letter. Adjust or reshape the child's fingers if the letter is incorrect. Do not be overly critical; you are not looking for perfection. As with anything else, a child's ability to form manual letters will improve in a sure, gradual way. At this early stage in a child's development, it is the internal kinesthetic feeling associated with isolating and identifying the individual letter that is important.

In the years to come, when the manual alphabet is firmly established, fingerspelling will become a useful memory tool for children learning how to spell or recall anything. But specifically for the baby or young child, who is learning how to speak, knowledge of the manual alphabet can become an aid in discriminating among beginning consonant sounds in a word. The manual alphabet comes into play in this way when a child is trying to express feelings and indicates a desire for something by using immature speech. The child may say something that sounds like *all*. You are unsure whether the child wants a ball or a doll. You can help distinguish between the two words by making the manual *b* and saying, Do you mean *ball*?, then making the manual *d* and asking, Do you mean *doll*? Because the visual acuity is developmentally ahead of their aural acuity, the child can distinguish between the manual *b* and the manual *d* more easily than the child can hear the difference between the oral *b* and oral *d*.

Using the manual alphabet in this way, as a tool to identify a referent, facilitates the child's ability to establish meaning and communicate in clear verbal English. Eliminating ambiguity and the confusion and frustration that often accompany it encourages the child to continue to attempt to speak and communicate. Success breeds more success.

The manual alphabet and fingerspelling can be a precursor to helping a child to recognize printed letters. They will firmly fix the idea in a child's mind that a sound can be represented in a physical form. By associating the sound with a specific letter, the manual alphabet becomes an effective transition to print. In addition, when the manual alphabet is used in this way, to connect a letter to the sound it represents, you are presenting early phonics lessons for tots.

In another situation, sign language is useful with young children in the home because of its facility to signify feelings in a quiet, understandable way. The feeling signs are nearly all iconic. Because the signs visually represent feelings in a discernible form, the child can comprehend the meaning of the word and relate the word to their own feelings. They are congruent. Children find it easier to identify their feelings, to express their feelings, to discuss their feelings, to understand their feelings, and to perform the same operations with the feelings of others.

During this chapter I have focused my attention on babies and young children. How can sign be used with older children in the home? What are the advantages or outcomes of including sign language in the day-to-day experience of ordinary school-age children?

To answer this question I am going to use the experience of a family who live in Oregon. In their community the public elementary school has closed. This occurred because many families were home schooling their children. The former school building is now used as a link-up center where the families go for a variety of enrichment classes. The course offerings cover a wide range of subjects from pottery to foreign languages. These include Spanish, French, and American Sign Language.

The family I am describing home schools their children. Jessica and Alexandra, their six- and seven-year-old daughters, attend sign language classes at the link-up center. The classes are for kindergarten-through sixth-grade-age children. They are held once a week, and a parent must accompany any child younger then ten. Therefore, the class has students as young as five and as old as the oldest parent. Often there are even children younger than five, when the baby or toddler siblings of class members join the group.

There are twenty children and five adults in the family's current class. This is the second year the family has been taking sign class together. They are very enthusiastic about learning sign language. One of the things they enjoy is being able to communicate with each other across a room when they are not close enough to talk to each other. Sign has come in handy in places where they are supposed to be quiet. By using sign language, they can ask questions and get answers without disturbing other people. For instance, one Sunday during their church service, the father could not locate one of the children and wondered what had happened to two-year-old Luke. After her father queried her in sign, Alexandra was able to sign back to him that Luke was asleep in the church's crying room.

The entire family had a grand time on a train trip from Portland to Seattle. They observed other passengers' signing and were able to communicate with them. The father thought this was a very positive experience for the children, and it has led to many family conversations about Deaf people, Deaf culture, and Deaf education. In addition to the obvious educational benefits they are all acquiring, the family has simply had fun with sign. They enjoy doing it together (P. Kazmierowicz, personal communication, November 16, 1999).

I have discussed the family class with their teacher, Diane Dennis. She also teaches ASL in the local junior and senior high school, where ASL is a language elective for which the students receive foreign language credit. She particularly appreciates the family class for its unique age-level aspect. Sometimes there are children, parents, and grandparents all learning sign together and having a ball doing it.

The very youngest children, often the toddler siblings of the grade-school children, are many times the best signers. Often a quiet, shy little three- or four-year-old child will sit on the floor and just observe the class. After a while she will notice that the child is beginning to form the signs silently. She believes sign is especially helpful for these shy children, for in her estimation knowing the sign gives them something special and they seem to blossom.

Diane strives to maintain ASL syntax, but this is not always easy to achieve. Many times the students place the signs in English word order and are actually doing signed English. She says the youngest members of the multiage class appear to find it easier to use ASL. She is not overly worried about this aspect, noting that they are all learning the ASL vocabulary and stressing that when students are in a daily ASL class, such as the high school class, they readily achieve the ASL syntax. In her estimation, the ASL vocabulary knowledge itself should prove useful to them and the syntax will come with more exposure (D. Dennis, personal communication, December 1, 1999).

I would like to close this chapter with some facts about the way all native languages are learned. In general they are not taught. They are assimilated in a natural fashion by infants and children from the language they encounter in the world about them. All children in the world acquire a complete language system in the same way, by the time they are five or six years old. No one teaches them the grammar or vocabulary. They encounter it and mimic it and assimilate it.

When children are raised in bilingual homes they learn both languages simultaneously in an easy fashion. In homes where the two languages are spoken such as English and French homes or English and Spanish homes, the children have no trouble code-switching from one language to the other language and grow up knowing both languages. It is the same way in the homes where ASL and English are used. The Deaf actress Marlee Matlin, who has an English-speaking husband, often describes how their baby understood and used her ASL as well as her husband's English and effortlessly became a truly bilingual child.

When you introduce sign language to your baby or young child in the home, you are simulating this natural condition. Of course, if you are just learning the sign and are not a fluent signer, you will not achieve the same results as a native signer or even a sign language interpreter. However, this level of language fluency is not your goal. You should be able to teach the child a basic ASL vocabulary and establish an early avenue of communication between parent and child, well before a child and parent can talk together.

Remember that babies understand much more than they are able to say. Speaking is difficult. It requires the development of dozens of muscles in the face, mouth, and tongue, and coordination of these muscles with the flow of the breath over the vocal folds in the larynx. From a purely developmental point of view, babies achieve the ability to construct language with their hands at least six to twelve months earlier than they do with their vocal apparatus.

But what of the language that they construct? When babies are able to say their first word, they produce the sound of the word, but what of the referent? Does the sound indicate the intended referent? The line between word and image is far easier to comprehend in sign language for both the sender and the receiver. This means that sign can help create meaning between parent and child, establish an early familial bond, and lead to better language development.

Sign can empower a young child as it eliminates the necessity to scream, cry, and generally carry on, because its communicative ability allows the child to express needs. This aspect apparently cultivates a strong sense of self-worth in youngsters and permits them to enjoy greater confidence. There have been many reports of this phenomenon throughout this book.

Become an early partner with your child as together you dance with the words of ASL. Both your fingers and hands and your child's fingers and hands can create meaning in the air as you silently exchange messages in sign language. For your child this dance will activate formative links in the developing brain; teach phonics, vocabulary, word recognition, and comprehension; become a precursor to the recognition of print; provoke positive feedback from others; give access to Deaf people; engender feelings of self-worth; and ultimately aid reading and spelling and communicative ability in general. It is a dance with words, to be enjoyed from babyhood, through childhood, to adulthood.

Index

activity centers, 35, 59

ADA (American with Disabilities Act), 15, 103, 166

ADD (Attention Deficit Disorder), 72, 124

American Academy of Child and Adolescent Psychiatry, 99

American manual alphabet
  description of, 145, 146
  to foster print awareness, 21, 25, 113, 170–172
  in games, 151, 159
  history of, 7, 12–13
  to teach
    alphabet, 44, 90, 113, 150
    letter names, 19, 35, 90, 113, 150
    letter sounds, 44, 90, 113, 152
    spelling, 160
  for writing, 126

American School for the Deaf, 89

Analco, Carol, 100–101

anchor thought, 125–126

ASL (American Sign Language)
  acquisition of by
    Deaf individuals, 13
    hearing adults, 15–16
    hearing children of Deaf parents, 78–83
    hearing children of interpreters, 79–80
    hearing infants, 9, 78–83
    hearing multi-age learners, 172–173
    hearing teachers, 43–44, 53
    young hearing students, 15–16
  assessment tool, 88, 150, 160, 162
  constructing signs, 13, 146
  courses in, 144–145, 165, 167–168, 173
  dictionary, 54, 144, 148, 167
  as a foreign language, 14–16, 62, 65, 72, 77, 134–135, 145, 166, 173